THE ASHES

RUGBY LEAGUE'S MOST IMPORTANT RIVALRY

BILLY ROBERTS

The Ashes - Rugby League's Most Important Rivalry

Copyright © 2025 Billy Roberts.

All rights reserved.

ISBN- 978-0-6459142-8-3 – Ebook
ISBN- 978-0-6459142-9-0 – Paperback

OTHER BOOKS BY THE AUTHOR

CROSSROADS - Rugby League's Greatest Battle

HillBilly Lessons for the Road -
Stuff They Never Taught You at School

CONTENTS

Other Books by the Author iii
Intro 1
Great Britain's Decline 17
Australia's Arrogance 34
The Fans' Growing Appetite 45
Tours - The Wow Event Factor 53
Scheduling 70
Financial Sustainability 81
Custodians for the International Game 93
Key Parties - France/Wales/New Zealand/Pacific Nations 100
Existential Crisis 119
Epilogue 123

INTRO

IN AUGUST 2023, the International Rugby League (IRL) finally announced a new schedule for the international game. The highlight of the announcement included the return of the England rugby league team to tour Australia in 2025, which was later amended in November 2024 with the announcement that Australia would instead tour the UK at the end of the 2025 season in what would be the first Ashes series since 2003. Incredibly, 2017 was the last time the two giants and grand rivals of world rugby league had played each other, with Australia defeating England in the Rugby League World Cup final 6-0 in a cracking game at Brisbane's Suncorp Stadium in front of 40,000 fans.

Eight years is an incredibly long gap for one of rugby league's greatest rivalries, that somehow seems to have been forgotten between the playing of the NRL and the Super League, the major competitions in both hemispheres.

Could you imagine the Ashes cricket series not being

played for 8 years or Australia not playing the All Blacks for 8 years in the rugby union Bledisloe Cup? But sadly, this scenario has occurred in rugby league and has been to the code's detriment and loss.

The last Ashes series is an even longer period of time, with the last three-game test series held way back in 2003 in the UK, and the last conventional longer format Kangaroo tour being held in 1994. Little did we know at the time that the fantastic '94 tour would be the end of an era for Ashes and rugby league tours.

The Ashes series was once the pinnacle of the code for both the northern and southern hemispheres. But this all started to slowly change in the 1980s when Australia's State of Origin series between New South Wales and Queensland exploded in popularity with emotion unmatched in Australian sport. Origin has now become the pinnacle for the sport Down Under, with huge crowds, massive media attention over the three-game series, and huge television ratings. The code's administrators have also had a weaker appetite for the international game (post Super League), with the NRL competition season and State of Origin taking all the focus, priority and scheduling in recent years, despite the NRL reaffirming verbally its long-term commitment to the international game in recent times. State of Origin has become a huge cash cow for the NRL, with the series reported to be worth well over $100 million annually and growing each year, and now has expanded well beyond the foundations of New South Wales and Queensland borders, with games now played around the country, including Melbourne, Perth and Adelaide in recent years. There is the strong possibility that the showpiece may be taken overseas in the future if the right money and publicity comes along, with England and New Zealand likely hosts if the game is ever taken abroad.

Despite the rise of Origin, beginning in the early 1980s in Australia, the 1982 and 1986 Kangaroo tours to the UK will long live in the folklore of the game, with the Kangaroos blitzing their British opposition to go through both tours undefeated and to be later called The Invincibles. This shocked the UK fans at the time, with many UK supporters believing the British had a strong chance to win both series before the tours started. They were later stunned at the skills, fitness and improvement of the Kangaroos, with a host of emerging Australian star players including Wally Lewis, Peter Sterling, Gene Miles, Mal Meninga, Brett Kenny and many more. Many experts believe the more professional approach from such coaches as the legendary Jack Gibson, who was heavily influenced by American professional sports in that time period, was a critical factor in the higher standards from the Kangaroos, and is a key reason for the growing gap in performance between Australia and Great Britain in the 1980s, compared to the 1970s.

In the early 1990s, the British game saw a revival of the sport, with the national team coming into full prominence across the mainstream media. Wigan had become the glamour team of world rugby league from the mid-1980s to the mid-1990s, being the dominant team and winning all the trophies available, and the success of their star-studded team filtered through to the national team. The UK game had a host of new stars who were well known to the general public, including Ellery Hanley, Martin Offiah, Gary Schofield, Shaun Edwards, Phil Clarke, Andy Farrell, Andy Platt, Jonathan Davies, Jason Robinson and Gary Connolly, to name just a few.

In Australia, the sport was also going through a boom period, with surging popularity under the strong leadership of John Quayle and Ken Arthurson, who had cleaned up the image of the sport after much criticism from many supporters for the thuggish on-field acts of the 1970s and 1980s. They expanded the competition, which included adding a host of new teams around Australia and New Zealand between 1988 and 1995, cultivated an attractive style of play for players and fans with the new 10-metre rule, signed a new television deal with the Nine Network media owner Kerry Packer, and created one of sport's greatest marketing campaigns in Simply the Best with star performer Tina Turner, taking the code to new levels not imaginable in the prior decades, with the code becoming the clear leader in Australian sport in many fans' and pundits' eyes.

Between 1990 and 1995, the two famous rivals of rugby league would write a new and exciting chapter in this long traditional rivalry, with the Great Britain Lions taking Game 1 of both the 1990 and 1994 Ashes series at Wembley, London in the UK with dramatic victories, before the Kangaroos would fight back to claim both the 1990 and 1994 series in tough and competitive series.

The Great Britain tour Down Under in 1992 would see the British push Australia all the way, which included their famous victory in Melbourne in Game 2 of the series, 33-10, before narrowly losing the decider in Brisbane, 22-16, before a full house at Lang Park. The teams would again meet at Wembley, London in the Rugby League World Cup final in late 1992 in front of over 73,000 fans, with Australia scoring a famous 10-6 win over Great Britain, Steve Renouf scoring the match winner in the dying minutes of the game after a superb outball pass from his Brisbane Bronco's teammate Kevin Walters to cut through the British defence.

1995 saw a bold, new and ambitious World Cup format hosted by England and Wales, with Great Britain returning to the home nation model for the tournament, with England and Wales both having teams in the expanded ten-team competition. Wales were boosted by a number of rugby union converts including Jonathan Davies, Scott Quinnell, Scott Gibbs, Allan Bateman, John Devereux, Jonathan Griffiths, Kevin Ellis and many other code hoppers, and had great success in the tournament, reaching the semi-finals before losing to England in front of 30,000 fans at Manchester's Old Trafford. The Welsh saw excellent crowds across the tournament and gained plenty of publicity, interest and support from the Welsh public in a renowned rugby union country.

Australia would be without its Super League stars for the tournament, who were refused eligibility by the ARL to play in the competition, creating enormous pressure for the remaining selected Kangaroo players to win the cup, with a host of star players missing from strong clubs like the Brisbane Broncos and Canberra Raiders. England would defeat Australia 20-16 in the opening game of the tournament, before the old rivals would once again meet in the final at Wembley, where Australia would take revenge and win 16-8 before a crowd of 66,540.

Little did many fans and followers of the code know at the time that the early to mid-90s revival of the Ashes and the international game would be the last great true modern period of this old rivalry, and that extended traditional Ashes tours both Down Under and across the UK would not be seen over the next 30 years, and both leagues would face perilous and chaotic times over the next 30 years to survive, and would see significant amount of change to their respective sporting league landscapes that continues to this day.

The code's greatest rivalry would never quite reach the lofty heights or momentum seen during the wonderful era of the early to mid-90s revival, despite international games still being played between 1996 and 2017, with many great test matches in this period, including the 2017 World Cup final. Condensed tours would replace extended Ashes tours for both 2001 and 2003, and international club games on tour would be a thing of the past. The UK Super League would move to a summer season model in 1996, there would be no fixed schedule for the international game for many years ahead, the tri nations and quad nations formats would replace full tours in some years, and mid-season series would not be seen again, with most international games moved to the end of the premiership season after the Kangaroos hammered Great Britain 64-10 in Sydney in 2002.

Australian rugby league was torn apart during the Super League war in the mid-1990s, with the civil war destroying the fabric of the game and causing many fans around the country to walk away from the game forever. The sport would never be the same again, with some scars still relevant today. The Super League war was all about pay television, with Ruper Murdoch wanting to introduce and expand his pay television network Foxtel into the Australian market, and no sport was more popular than rugby league at the time. Murdoch knew he needed a product to entice Australians to buy Foxtel and knew no sport was more suited or qualified than rugby league, with its huge television audience and growing popularity across Australia. The many governance failures and the club's legal contractual failures left the ARL and rugby league open to being attacked by Murdoch and to create a new competition, and this was further fueled with the rogue and ambitious Brisbane Broncos clashing with the ARL head office over the running of the game before the war started. The civil war would reach its peak with separate competitions in 1997 before a reunification merged league under the NRL banner was introduced in 1998.

The healing and recovery has been a long and slow process since the Super League war started, with split competitions and newly merged competitions to create the NRL from the ashes of the ARL and Super League competitions. Teams would be axed, new teams would join the competition, such as Melbourne Storm in 1998, Gold Coast Titans in 2007, and Dolphins in 2023, with new teams still to come from Perth (2027) and Papua New Guinea in (2028). Club mergers would occur, with many foundation clubs forced to merge. There would be huge conflicts of interest, with a media company now owning half the game post Super League when the

NRL was created, major governance failures, the formation of an independent governing body to administer the sport in 2012, the Australian Rugby League Commission (ARLC), perilous financial issues, COVID, and now the code looking at once again going back down the strategic path that John Quayle and Ken Arthurson were slowly implementing in the early to mid-1990s before the Super League war erupted and tore the game apart.

Today, the NRL is the second strongest league in the Australian sporting market, with improved finances, favourable TV ratings and growing crowds in recent times after COVID pressures, and has a dominant position in the NSW and QLD markets and a growing presence in Victoria, with Melbourne Storm's long run of success since its inception. Despite the strong television ratings, improved finances and growing crowd numbers in recent seasons, there are still many lingering issues underneath the professional level, with the community and country game seeing a drop in player numbers and overall interest in the last decade or longer, which is a threat to the code's long-term success in Australia. Many fans are now also growing increasingly concerned about the mass influence of gambling across the game, with the code's integrity becoming a rising concern. The many new rules introduced, such as the six again rule, only fuel concerns about the integrity of the sport when games can be easily manipulated, and it only seems a matter of time before a major gambling scandal emerges for the code.

The NRL has also been embroiled in a number of conflict of interest matters in recent years that has further eroded the trust of many fans, involving a number of high-profile media representatives, media companies, the NRL, and NRL clubs.

Long-term media deals have secured the code good revenue post COVID, as the code has invested in a variety of assets such as pubs and motels, and the women's game has seen significant growth in a short space of time. In addition, the games stadiums at many NRL clubs have improved significantly, to further boost crowd attendances in recent years and upgrade facilities for fans and sponsors. State of Origin continues to be the prized jewel in the crown, with games, as mentioned, now being shared across the country, with Adelaide, Perth and Melbourne all hosting games, and a growing share of the Pacific market fanbase at home and abroad from the once dominant rugby union Polynesian and Pacific market. New Zealand has seen a second wave of popularity for the code in its homeland, with the New Zealand Warriors surging in popularity across the country. This level of support has not been seen since their entry into the Australian Rugby League (ARL) in 1995.

The NRL has also been very aggressive with future expansion plans, with the Perth Bears to join the NRL from 2027 and a Papua New Guinea team to enter the league in 2028, after huge financial support was guaranteed by the Anthony Albanese Labor Government. The deal was approved after geopolitical threats from China helped secure Papua New Guinea's entry into the NRL, despite plenty of national criticism over the decision.

The UK game has faced its own significant challenges since the 1995 Rugby League World Cup, with initial cash flow problems as the game turned professional, which led to the signing with Rupert Murdoch's BSkyB and the creation of the brand Super League and a move to summer from winter, which would impact the old rivalry with the Ashes, with scheduling clashes for both competitions. This has also led to narrowing the opportunity for meaningful international tours, with seasons now running in alignment for both leagues.

Despite the initial injection of cash from Sky Sports in a deal brokered by the legendary Maurice Lindsay, the UK game has lost many fans over the last 30 years and has become only a minor sport in the UK. It went behind pay television walls in 1996 with the Sky Sports deal and seems to be unsure of how to move the game forward and reinvigorate itself with the wider public, with many sports now moving ahead of rugby league in the UK pecking order. The game's governance model has come under heavy criticism in recent years, with a belief that the big Super League club owners are controlling the game with their own vested interests, whilst the lower level and amateur clubs believe they have been forgotten and have little say in the future and the running of the sport. Super League owners would take more control of the competition in 2018 under CEO Robert Elstone, after a split with the governing body, RFL (Rugby Football League), after the RFL came under heavy criticism for its poor running of the sport, lack of profile, declining playing numbers and crowds, and financial mismanagement from many Super League club owners.

This led to much anger from fans and clubs across the sport, who believed the wealthy club owners were only looking out for their own vested interests and not the greater game, with many calling out the selfishness of some clubs and owners. There were also the huge governance failures, with the split factions allowing clubs to take control of Super League and leaving the RFL to administer the rest of the sport.

In March 2022 at a special general meeting, it was announced the RFL and Super League would officially realign, but so far there has been no happy ending to the division between key stakeholders, with Super League clubs pushing to remove RFL president Simon Johnson in 2025, to be replaced by former RFL CEO Nigel Wood.

Many fans and stakeholders have also been very critical of the RFL's performance, with many blaming the governing body for the code's decline and the reason why Super League club owners wanted total control of the sport, after losing faith and confidence in the RFL to drive the game forward both on and off the field.

With both the RFL and Super League club owners unable to change the direction of the game in recent times, continuing with a governance model that had no real unity, fairness, absolute power, structure or cohesion, the RFL and Super League would later sign a deal with IMG in 2022 to reimagine the sport after years of decline, and remodel the game with a newly created grading system, plus other changes all hoped to improve the sport. The RFL is reported to be paying in excess of £450k per annum in a 12-year agreement, with the first two years gratis.

IMG, originally known as the International Management Group, is a global sports, fashion, events and media company headquartered in New York City. The company manages athletes and fashion celebrities; owns, operates and commercially represents live events; and is an independent producer and distributor of sports and entertainment media.

IMG have worked with such sports as golf, soccer, tennis, UFC, athletics and many other sports around the world.

Many fans and experts within the game have been disappointed thus far with IMG's results, with criticism of the grading model and the scoring system, the removal of relegation and promotion, the sports media deals, continued lack of profile, declining revenues, lack of true stars, and the current direction for the sport.

The RFL, Super League and IMG deal is a 12-year partnership, but the direction of the sport is still plagued with governance, economic and decision-making issues, with one unsure who is really running the game. There are so many stakeholders now involved across the British game, where the NRL governance model has the commission as the head of the sport, with elected commissioners overseeing the strategic direction for the game at all levels, and the NRL clubs and state bodies sitting under this structure. There is no doubt that the IMG has a tough job ahead if they are to fulfill their mission of reimagining the sport, especially if they don't have full support or the decision-making power and authority to do so. The grading system both on and off the field is probably needed to raise standards across the game, as they look to raise the profile, despite the many critics. But this has also clashed with the history and tradition of the sport across the UK.

With a tremendous on-field product and many great clubs with a long and proud history in the north of England, the

British game should be far more popular and in a much better position than where it finds itself in 2025. The off-field management and governance of the British game has been terrible, and the game now pays a heavy price, with declining revenues from major broadcaster Sky and little interest elsewhere to fill the void, smaller grand final crowds compared to its peak, lower playing numbers, and a sport that seems to be facing an existential and identity crisis. This was again highlighted when the clubs voted out RFL president Simon Johnson in March 2025, bringing back Nigel Wood as interim leader in another boardroom scandal, which again highlighted the division between key stakeholders across the British rugby league landscape.

St Helens Chairman Eamonn McManus, in an interview with Sky Sports in early 2025, said Super League clubs were losing millions each year and could not continue to lose this type of money each season and expect to be bailed out by rich club owners. He stated television revenue from Sky had continued to decline significantly from its peak, and there was no way this could continue, moving forward.

London Broncos were one of the most harshly treated clubs, despite its very strategic importance to the British game in the capital, under the new IMG grading system for promotion and relegation, starting in 2025. They won promotion to the Super League in 2024 from the Rugby League Championship competition in 2023, after defeating Toulouse 18-14 in the final in 2023 in Toulouse, France, against all odds. The club did not spend anywhere near the salary cap limit for 2024, despite being promoted, after being graded far lower by IMG than most other clubs before a ball had even been kicked at the start of 2024, to remain in Super League for 2025. It was clear the Broncos would be graded lower and with relegation to be scrapped, no matter what happened on the field in 2024, a long-held tradition in the game. They would be back in the lower tier Championship for the 2025 season and have to start the long climb again to re-enter Super League.

In early 2025, it was announced that Salford Red Devils were in major financial stress and would need forward club payments and have to offload players to survive. Salford's precarious position made a mockery of the IMG gradings, with Salford included in the top 12 clubs in the Super League grading system, despite being under severe financial stress. Sadly, they will not be the last club in this position, as economic conditions continue to be difficult, and less revenue is coming into the game. Many UK clubs at all levels can only survive with wealthy owners, but one questions the sustainability of such a model long term. One could say it is quite similar to the current scene for the Australian music festivals, where we have seen many big iconic festivals such as Splendour in the Grass and the Blues Fest in Byron Bay collapse due to a variety of economic issues, making the festivals unprofitable and too risky for many promoters and investors, who carry the financial risk with any event. Meanwhile, the Tamworth Country Music Festival thrives with a different business model, where the risk is spread across many venues and locations, with free entry to many music performances and not being dependent on a small or single group of major investors and promoters. It is now bringing in hundreds of thousands to the event each year and has become the biggest music festival in Australia, continuing to grow each year.

Whilst the NRL is currently a much stronger league today both financially and in popularity compared with the British Super League, both competitions need each other and really are strong allies for each league and the greater game itself, and are not rivals off the pitch, as many have believed. The NRL's invitation to include Super League clubs Wigan and Warrington in Las Vegas for the season opener in 2025 and Leeds and Hull KR for 2026 is ample proof of the benefit for both leagues working together to grow the game across both the northern and southern hemisphere, and to build deeper ties and commercial benefits. It was reported that over 10,000 UK fans attended the Las Vegas event in 2025, and the 2026 event has already seen strong ticket sales involving Hull KR and Leeds.

While much has happened on and off the field over the last 30 years in both the UK and Australia, this book is all about ensuring and advocating for the return of the grandest old rivalry in rugby league, the Ashes. The 2025 Ashes series is hopefully just the beginning of a new and exciting era of test match rugby league between the countries, that will hopefully continue on for many future generations to enjoy and honour a proud and long tradition in the game that goes all the way back to 1908.

Australia against England or Great Britain must be preserved, treasured and ensured its rightful place on the rugby league calendar to continue this long and proud history of the game and the legacy of this great rivalry.

The longer traditional tours must return in some format, even if they are shorter length tours with fewer games. The magic of past Ashes tours with Kangaroos tour games against UK clubs such as Wigan, St Helens, and Leeds, and the Lions tours Down Under with games against country teams and NRL clubs have left incredible memories for many supporters, and is a huge hole in the game that nothing has come close to filling since, despite the NRL and Super League extended season schedule. The Ashes and extended tours are one of the few wow factor events the game has, with an incredible history and legacy. The game has this at its disposal and yet it has sat on the shelf for over 20 years now, forgotten, which is just so sad and such a huge loss to the sport.

The game must continue to honour the past to ensure its future. A sport that forgets its past is in trouble, and sooner or later will face an identity or existential crisis in one form or another. One could argue today that both leagues are facing this issue and need each other to survive and prosper in ways they probably could not imagine or understand.

Australia against England is the greatest rivalry in the code, and nothing will ever come close to this, including State of Origin or any club rivalry from either competition. It must be preserved at all costs. Never more than now do both nations and competitions need this rivalry to prosper for themselves and the overall good of the game around the world.

GREAT BRITAIN'S DECLINE

ONE OF THE major reasons for the lack of appetite, interest and passion for international rugby league and in particular the revival of the Ashes series is that Great Britain or England have not won an Ashes series since 1970 or a World Cup since 1972. This is definitely the case and opinion for many Australian fans and administrators, who have had no real hatred or dislike for the Poms, and particularly for newer and younger fans of the sport, due to such a long run of dominance by the Kangaroos (now over 50 years), plus the inactivity of international competition in more recent times, especially Ashes tests. The passion between both nations has dwindled from what once was a burning flame of raw emotion unmatched, into just a candlestick now, if you compare this to what once was, or compared to the passion we now see between Australia and England in the Ashes cricket, which has seen some brilliant series over the two decades. It has had both sets of fans on the edge of their seat across the five-game test series, and has gone right to the end on a number of occasions with emotions and passion on display from players, commentators and fans.

Since Great Britain's last Ashes series win in 1970, Australia has played England or Great Britain in 13 series, with Australia winning them all including 3-0 in five of those series. The head-to-head count in Ashes series since 1970 is 39 games, with Australia winning 31 times compared to Great Britain/England eight times. Great Britain's last victory against the Kangaroos came all the way back in 2006 with their famous 23-12 win in the Tri Nations tournament at the Sydney Football Stadium, now some 19 years ago! England's last victory against the Kangaroos is even further back, with a 20-16 victory in the opening game of the 1995 World Cup at Wembley, London, an incredible 30 years ago now!

Since the first Ashes series in 1908 there have been 39 Ashes series, with Australia winning 20 series and Great Britain 19. The total games played were 118, with 59 Australia wins, 54 Great Britain wins, and five draws.

All great rivalries need two to make a great dance, and sport has had many great rivalries: the Lakers and Celtics, Agassi and Sampras, Djokovic and Federer, Nadal vs Federer, Djokovic vs Nadal, Bowe and Holyfield, NSW and QLD, Manchester United vs Liverpool, Glasgow Rangers vs Celtic, Frazier and Ali, Redsox vs Yankees, and the All Blacks vs the Springboks are just some of sport's best and most intense rivalries.

The only way the Ashes in rugby league can rise again and be restored to its rightful place as the pinnacle for the code is for Great Britain or England to defeat Australia in an Ashes series and for fans from both countries to respect and dislike each other, like all great rivalries. World War Two General Douglas MacArthur said, *"There is no substitute for victory,"* and nothing other than the British defeating the Kangaroos will count to revitalise the British and international game. Close enough is no longer good enough, and only victory in a World Cup final or Ashes series against Australia can restore this great rivalry to its rightful place at the top of rugby league and add an exciting and bright new future for the code and ensure administrators and leaders of the sport know of its vital importance and potential for many years to come.

The British game has been in a funk for many years now and the code's fanbase has declined in recent years, with access to Super League games being only behind paywalls on Sky Sports until recently, with a few games being shown now on free-to-air outside the Challenge Cup, for which the BBC provides free-to-air coverage. Many UK writers say the code has no real household names anymore and today's current players are unknown to the greater public, with the exception of the retired and late Rob Burrow, who sadly passed away in 2024, a true patriot in his fight for charity and raising awareness for MND (motor neurone disease). At the time of his death, Burrow would probably have been the code's most well known personality, having retired from the sport in 2017.

Soccer, cricket, rugby union, darts, tennis, UFC, boxing and golf all have many household names across the UK sporting landscape.

In simple terms, the British game badly needs star players

who are well known across the UK, who can raise the profile of the sport. Only by defeating Australia in high-profile test matches and series can the stars rise to the occasion and become household names in the media and across the UK landscape. The best against the best always attracts attention, no matter what sport it may be.

As mentioned earlier, the British game had a renaissance in the early 90s and there was a host of star players who were well known to the greater public when access to games was far easier than it is today, with such players as Ellery Hanley, Martin Offiah, Phil Clarke, Andy Farrell, Shaun Edwards, and Gary Schofield all well known to the British public. The British team from that era may not have won an Ashes series or World Cup, but they certainly pushed Australia all the way and won some incredible test matches in this golden period of international rugby league. But to really revitalise the international game and this grand rivalry, they need to go a step further and break the now 50 plus years hoodoo against the Aussies and create a whole new rivalry that will inspire current and future generations for many years to come.

In recent years, many believe the NRL competition has become far superior to its UK counterpart, the Super League, in terms of skill, quality, fitness, and talent, and the gap is only getting bigger, with many British players now being raided by NRL clubs with the huge money on offer Down Under. Never before have we seen so many British players in the NRL as there are today: Dom Young, Morgan Smithies, Herbie Farnworth, John Bateman, Kai Pearce Paul, Lewis Dodd, and

Matty Nicholson are just a few who have made the move from the Super League to the NRL in recent years.

Some of Britain's best modern players have plied their trade in the NRL era, including Sam Burgess, George Burgess, Tom Burgess, Adrian Morley, James Graham, Gareth Ellis, Gareth Widdop, George Williams, and Elliot Whitehead, to name just a few.

It used to be the other way around, where many Australian players would head to the UK, especially when the football seasons were not in sync, with the 1980s seeing a wave of Australian superstars play for English clubs, including Peter Sterling, Brett Kenny, Wally Lewis, Mal Meninga and many more players of international calibre.

There is great fear from many supporters of the British game that it will soon become a nursery for the NRL competition, and unless things change fast, that more and more of their best players will continue to leave the UK game for the NRL, which has far more money and public attention on offer for British players today.

The NRL has left the Super League for dead in terms of money, power and brand recognition, with the NRL's recent television deals far bigger than the Super League media deals, plus larger sponsorships, bigger attendances, more government support, better stadiums and the cash cow in State of Origin leaving the Super league and UK game in its wake.

The NRL earned $745 million in 2024 with the RFL making an audited loss in 2024 of £507,000, on a turnover of £13.52 million, down from £15.04 million in 2023.

Super League earnings from broadcaster Sky have continued to decline for the sport in recent years, with the 2024 media deal with Sky Sports worth £21.5 million, down from £40 million in 2021.

The NRL continues to build more cash reserves and an asset base far greater than the Super League and RFL, despite being in big trouble when COVID hit Australia in early 2020, when the game was at huge risk if games could no longer be played due to the pandemic, holding little cash reserves in 2020 if the games were postponed for an extended period of time, which looked highly likely in early 2020 and during parts of 2021, when both seasons were interrupted.

The NRL has since invested in pubs and motels, adding more cash reserves to the balance sheet since COVID to build its asset base, after having few assets when COVID first struck Australia in 2020. Chairman Peter V'Landys was clear that the game must build an emergency fund of cash and assets to ensure the code never finds itself in such a precarious position again, after hundreds of millions had passed through the game's hands before the pandemic with no investment or assets to show for it.

The British game now faces a league falling quickly behind the NRL both on and off the field. More and more star players are leaving Super League clubs for the NRL, there is a growing gulf in talent and playing standards according to many experts, numerous clubs are struggling financially, and there are ongoing governance issues and infighting between various stakeholders, which continues to divide the game between clubs at all levels, wealthy club owners, IMG, the RFL, players and supporters. The old adage that a house divided against itself cannot stand is evident in the British game we see today.

Many critics of the Super League and the UK game in general believe the competition has recruited far too many overpaid Australian and overseas players who are at the end of their playing career and are looking for one big final retirement pay cheque, and this has blocked the opportunities and progression for many of the best young British players, when Super League clubs pick more experienced Australians, New Zealanders and Pacific Islanders to ensure success, rather than the longer and more difficult process of developing players. This is even more so when clubs have had a fight to stay in Super League when facing a relegation battle.

My opinion is the British game has accepted far too many average imports from the NRL and this has affected the national team, the sports profile and the standard of the league. Overseas imports can be a very healthy addition and can increase the profile and playing standard, but the balance has tipped too far, with too many average imports for some clubs. This is the opinion of many ex-players in the UK including former Great Britain Captain Gary Schofield, who has been one of the biggest critics in recent years of the many overseas signings.

Despite the influx of overseas players, many British clubs have some great youth and pathway systems and have great talent coming through at clubs such as St Helens, Wigan, Warrington, Hull FC and Leeds.

This was evident in 2018 when the England Academy defeated the Australian Schoolboys 2-0, which included Jack

Welsby and Harry Smith, who have now become big stars for the British game in Super League. A number of other players have also emerged from this team in Super League including Harry Newman, Ethan Havard, Sam Walters, Owen Trout, Tom Holroyd, Innes and Louis Senior, and Morgan Smithies in the NRL, now with the Canberra Raiders, and many other players who have made the grade to Super League. The Australian Schoolboys team included Stephen Critchon, Tom Deardon, Bradman Best, Tommy Talau, and Jason Saab, to outline how strong England performed to win the series and that they do indeed have talent in the junior age groups to compete with any nation in the world. More overseas quotas for Super League, as approved for 2026, is not the solution, when we see quality players of this ilk from the 2018 English Academy team now becoming quality Super League players, who just need time to develop.

The success of Wigan Warriors in 2024 should be a blueprint for the UK game. They have recruited high quality overseas players in Bevan French and Jai Field, who were undervalued and both still in their prime. Wigan has also developed clear pathways for local players to make their way to the top team, with Junior Nsemba, Zach Eckersley and Harry Smith all making their way through the local pathway system and making a huge impression in 2024, as the club won all four trophies on offer, including the World Club Challenge, Challenge Cup, League Leaders Shield and Super League title, to cap off an incredible season for the Cherry and Whites.

Top-notch high profile players who have left the NRL to play in the Super League are great for the British game but are becoming more rare, with the money on offer far greater in the NRL today. However, Super League has still seen some great players make the switch from the NRL including Jamie Lyon, Allan Langer, Andrew Johns, Matt Gidley, David Fairleigh, Trent Barrett, Bevan French, Jared Waerea-Hargreaves, Joe Vagana, and Lesley Vainikolo, to name just a few who have lit up Super League and improved the overall standard and product and raised the profile for the game. But sadly, way too many Super League clubs have recruited too many washed-up ex NRL-players, which has blocked emerging British talent and not helped the national team with greater playing depth or attracted new fans to the game.

More and more Super League clubs have gotten smarter with recruitment with hiring more younger NRL players who have not cemented an NRL contract and who have untapped potential. Players such as Jai Field, Kai O'Donnell, and Tom Amone have all done really well in Super League, adding great value to their clubs and the league in general.

The All Blacks' long run of success in rugby union leaves many success clues, with everything in the system feeding into the All Blacks teams from the bottom up. This starts with schools and juniors, with the talented kids then going on to pathway programmes and then representative teams, then the semi-professional Mitre 10 competition (now the Bunnings Cup), which then feeds into the five Super Rugby franchises which are all owned by NZR (Auckland Blues, Wellington Hurricanes, Waikato Chiefs, Otago Highlanders and Canterbury Crusaders), which then feeds into the famous black jersey of the All Blacks. The Super Rugby teams are nearly all made up of NZ talent and have very few non-New Zealand players other than Pacific Island players, with the sole purpose to feed into the All Blacks programme and guarantee success with a greater playing pool and more depth across many positions.

The whole system is one big pathway to the All Blacks, and the national team's long run of success is one of the key priorities in the sport for senior leaders and fans alike. You can see why they have had such great success over the last 20 plus years with such focus, decisiveness and clear priorities. Compare this to the UK Rugby League, which is a mixed bag that is not in harmony at all, where there is a solid junior pathway from some clubs and the RFL, a struggling school system that needs more help, a community game that is losing player numbers, indecision on the structure of a reserve grade competition, the Betfred Rugby League Championship and League One, and then the big one Super League where clubs do not feed the national team as a priority. In fact, many of the Super League clubs and their owners are not supportive of international rugby league if that means their star players could get injured or miss some club games. Many Super League clubs care little for the national team and only their own clubs, and yet the code doesn't even have a regular scheduled international itinerary that clashes with club games. The NZ Rugby Union ecosystem works in harmony, from under 6's to the All Blacks, whereas the UK system is one big mess, and this has shown in the results over the last 50 plus years, despite valiant efforts from many players and coaches during this time.

Great Britain's Decline

A successful England or Great Britain Lions team is essential if the code wishes to reverse the downward trend many believe the British game is on. Nothing can attract national media attention and grow the profile of the sport like England or Great Britain Lions playing and winning meaningful test series against Australia or a World Cup both at home or abroad. Only a Super League grand final or Challenge Cup final can get anywhere near this coverage for the sport, but they come nowhere near a national team in major games where all the fans and clubs unite under one cause, flag, jersey and belief, and the attention becomes far greater and deeper.

Great Britain or England's national team must be at the centrepiece and heart and soul of the code, as a strategic and commercial priority for the future of the sport from IMG, Super League clubs and the RFL, if we are to see another renaissance of the British game. Despite the many doomsayers and critics across the UK game today, this is very possible if leaders of the code have a grand vision, some belief, and dogged persistence, and work in complete sync and harmony together to raise the sport again, with the code's best interests at heart.

As mentioned, rugby league in the UK faces some major challenges. Some of the major risks to the code's future are:

- Governance structure
- Financial sustainability for both clubs and the league
- TV revenue declining at an alarming rate
- Declining fan base

- Lack of growth and expansion
- Lack of profile in major cities such as London, Paris, and Cardiff
- The international game inactivity
- Playing standard and depth
- Championship and League One structure
- Promotion and relegation or direct appointment licences
- Attracting more fans and increasing profile
- Lack of star players well known to the British public

If the code is to change course, Great Britain's and England's success and rebranding must be central to the code's overall success and revival. Their success would filter through the whole sport from top to bottom, from encouraging more kids to play the sport and emulate their British heroes, improve the standard of Super League and its profile with better players, create more household names across the UK sporting landscape, larger crowds with more stars, bigger media deals with more eyes on the game, bigger sponsorship opportunities, a higher profile, and provide the governance model with a central theme to anchor the sport that can unite the whole sport from the community game to the professional top-tier Super league.

As you can see, it's a giant circle: Great Britain's and England's success feeds the whole ecosystem, but sadly, many involved in the sport do not see this today, and too often, many major stakeholders put selfish agendas before the sport's best interest. We clearly see the impacts of this attitude and philosophy over the last 30 to 50 years by the results on and off the field.

Look at the momentum, revenue, profile and publicity other English national teams have brought to their respective codes: soccer, rugby union and cricket being prime examples, whilst rugby league has left a huge void, with too much inactivity and indecision in missing so many opportunities, including major revenue opportunities and mainstream attraction to grow the sport's profile, allowing other sports to make huge gains during this period.

In many ways, the British game today is facing an existential crisis, not being sure how to move forward, what it is as a sport, how to honour its past and serve a diverse range of stakeholders from the amateur game to the professional level, how to attract new fans and compete with other major sports and ensure financial growth and stability, and find real meaning and purpose for the sport.

Great Britain Lions/England are a key element to finding meaning and purpose for the sport to honour the past and present, become a stable anchor across the game, and a key for the sport's future success and foundation. England or the Great Britain Lions should be seen as the pinnacle for those involved with the game in the UK.

I, for one, love the Super League competition and have loved it since I was a kid, when Foxtel would show a few Super League games every week in Australia. I instantly loved

Eddie and Stevo's passionate commentary, the loud crowds, the unique style of play and how it was so different to the NRL, and in many ways so much better to watch, with more emotion and drama. Nothing has changed for me as a fan of the British game.

While the NRL may have more money and attention, with bigger television deals and other sources of revenue, I find the Australian sport has become flooded with gambling influences and new rules such as the six again, captain's challenge and video referee interference, which has impacted the viewing quality, despite the sport's enormous popularity in New South Wales and Queensland. Players in the NRL today may be bigger, faster and fitter than ever before, but this does not equate to a better viewing product, and I find nearly all the teams play with the same style and routine, and lack imagination, with the game becoming heavily offence oriented, despite the strong modern influence of MMA and wrestling, with the code moving more towards a mix of tag and touch rugby, although many newer fans love this fast-paced style of play and the many similar body shapes of modern players.

I firmly believe there needs to be a balance between attack and defence and to offer opportunities for all shapes and sizes, but the NRL is definitely going more for speed and offence, trying to please the modern fans.

Super League and the UK game have a unique niche in the northern hemisphere and they should not just follow or copy whatever the NRL does. We have seen this trend continue with rule changes such as the six again introduction, captain's

Great Britain's Decline

challenge for 2025 and the removal of relegation from 2024 for Super League.

The UK game was born in Huddersfield in 1895 when a group of clubs broke away from rugby union, and was there before rugby league commenced in Australia in 1908. It should forge its own path and not just follow what the NRL does every time and play copycat, despite many stakeholders in the British game wanting the NRL to take full control and ownership of Super League.

I remember Wayne Bennett saying to the media when coaching the English national team that the players had a belief problem and this would need to be fixed if they were to ever defeat Australia. He said the players had all the physical capabilities, but were lacking in the mental department, and unless this changed, they would never beat Australia.

I, for one, believe in the Super League and the game both on and off the field in the UK in general, despite many of the code's current issues that continue to plague the code. I am sure that Super League can become one of the premier sporting competitions in the UK and the world. They currently have a playing group that has the potential to break the 50 plus years hoodoo and defeat Australia.

Jack Welsby, Herbie Farnworth, Junior Nsemba, Zach Eckersley, Tom Holroyd, Harry Smith, Mikey Lewis, and Dom Young are all young, exciting and exceptionally talented rugby league players. The sport's leaders must believe in this group and rebuild the England and Great Britain team around such a core group of players.

Many say the Super League is well behind the NRL in

depth and quality, but it would only take one special group to change the fortunes of the past and create a whole new exciting future for the British game and international rugby league.

The Michael Vaughan era, as leader of the English cricket team, is a perfect example of how fast positive change can happen and how the ripple effect can quickly spread across the whole sport from top to bottom, with Australia's dominance against England teams in the years before Vaughan took the national team's captaincy.

The 2023 and 2024 World Club Challenge victories for St Helens and Wigan over Penrith both at home and abroad should provide the code and the British game with plenty of optimism that England can have success in the 2025 Ashes series. It just needs belief and a stoic mindset from the players and coaches involved.

The 2025 Ashes series in the UK is much more than just another series for the British. The British game badly needs success to help boost the code and morale across the entire game, and nothing can help it more than England's success in the 2025 Ashes series. It can create momentum and opportunity that nothing else in the sport can match.

The British will be heavy underdogs to reclaim the Ashes and will be written off by the Australian public and media, but this squad has the potential, under experienced coach Shaun Wane, to do the impossible and shock the rugby league world.

Great Britain's and England's decline and inactivity has hurt the sport, the international game and Super League significantly, and it must be central to the code's health and revival if we are to see another renaissance and revival of the

British game that so many fans and supporters long for and wish to see again.

A successful England or Great Britain team is essential to any future for the sport, plus upholding and continuing the traditions and prestige of the Ashes series.

Destiny is now in the hands of the British.

AUSTRALIA'S ARROGANCE

NO COUNTRY HAS held back the progress of the international game and in particular the rivalry between Australia and England/Great Britain more so than Australia and the NRL post Super League.

Contrary to popular opinion, the NRL has had a lackadaisical attitude towards developing and promoting the international game over the last 20 plus years, and no amount of words from head office can hide this. Actions are always your best indicator, and the talk from the NRL does not match in deeds, despite some recent action in the last few years to promote and support the international game in the Pacific, and the major tour announcement of the Kangaroos to tour the UK in 2025 to play the first Ashes series since 2003.

Australia, which has the strongest competition in world rugby league with the NRL, should be the leaders in promoting the sport internationally, but instead, they have at times been the worst offenders for sabotaging and not supporting the international game's growth.

The NRL cancelled the 2021 Rugby League World Cup at extremely short notice, blaming COVID, causing the whole competition to be delayed for 12 months, despite other sports playing internationals in the UK in the same time period, with the overwhelming majority of other nations willing to play in the tournament and the NRL players all wanting to play. Various polls confirmed this when the media released the players' polling results. The players were not consulted, according to the players union and numerous media reports. The decision to cancel the 2021 Rugby League World Cup was made by the ARLC and NRL clubs without consultation with the players, despite pleas from the host organisers for the tournament to go ahead in 2021, after many years of preparation and hard work for such an event.

Peter V'landys made one of the most arrogant comments ever, after confirming Australia would not attend the World Cup, despite the pleas of cup organisers, who had spent years in preparation to host the event.

V'landys arrogantly stated, *"I was surprised. I think they thought we were convicts in our prisoner outfits."*

That remark may go down as one of the most ignorant, arrogant and egotistical comments from any leader in the history of the game. Event organisers had poured many years of time, effort and money into organising the event. Players from other countries, many not professional, had sacrificed much in preparation for the event, and yet that did little to stop V'landys taking a swipe at his critics. It only exposed his arrogance and his lack of understanding and historical knowledge of the international game, and the selfish attitude of the NRL and its clubs.

It's not just the cancellation on late notice of the 2021 Rugby League World Cup. Australia has a long list of not supporting the international game and continuing the rivalry with Great Britain/England despite the Pacific Championships being played at the end of the NRL season in recent years across the Pacific.

In 2001, the Kangaroos were not going to tour the UK and play in the Ashes, and were only persuaded by legendary UK administrator Maurice Lindsay, who pleaded for the Kangaroos to tour or the British game would face financial ruin, after the September 11 attacks in New York. The Kangaroos eventually agreed to tour but would play only the three test matches and no other tour games.

The last proper Ashes series was played in 2003, despite many pleas from the British officials for tours to be played between the two nations since then.

Australia declined to tour England in 2020, despite pleas from British representatives, with Australia blaming COVID for the cancellation of the series and being called lackadaisical about the Ashes legacy from the English.

The NRL competition schedule continues to run longer and longer each year, with the 2024 NRL season running over 27 rounds, which excludes pre-season trials and a final series, meaning the game now runs from around early February to early October. This does not include pre-season training, leaving very little space for the international game and a proper Ashes series, especially in Australia, where cricket takes over in the summer months and the weather becomes much warmer and is not suited for quality rugby league. Many Australian fans also tend to switch off after the NRL grand final and move to cricket, and the ratings have proven this, with many international games rating lower post the regular season, despite strong ratings for the Pacific Cup in late 2024.

Some may say the NRL has done an excellent job in promoting the game in the Pacific region in recent years, but I would challenge this opinion, and want to understand better what carrots are really being thrown to the NRL from the Australian Government to support the game in a number of Pacific nations.

The Pacific region has become a very political topic in recent years, with China's deep push into the region via the belt and road initiative, which the Australian Government and its international allies fear. The Labor Government has worked with a number of sports, in particular, the NRL, to support initiatives that promote cohesion and brotherhood between Australia and Pacific nations such as Papua New Guinea, Fiji, Tonga, the Cook Islands and Samoa.

The current government has promised enormous amounts of funding for the next NRL franchise from Papua New Guinea. This has nothing to do with sport or the NRL and is all about politics. The NRL, I believe, are chasing the money rather than doing what is best for the sport and its long-term strategic plan, despite the many supporters for a team from PNG. In Australia, the NRL needs to remain close to the elected government officials to benefit from tax exemptions, stadium upgrades across the country, sponsorship for major events such as State of Origin, the Brisbane Magic Weekend and the grand final, which many fans are not aware of, which is a huge source of revenue and assets upgrades for the game.

It's all about money and politics, and whilst PNG has legitimate claims to be an expansion team in the NRL, there is no doubt they were behind other regions on many key metrics such as Perth, a second NZ team, more Queensland teams and possibly even an Adelaide team.

On 12 December 2024, the Labor Government, with the Prime Minister Anthony Albanese alongside the PNG Prime Minister James Marape and ARLC Chairman Peter V'landys, announced that Papua New Guinea would be granted entry into the NRL from 2028 with a deal worth an incredible $600 million in funding to support the new team. The announcement was received with a mixed response, with plenty of vocal criticism that the government would fund such large amounts of money during the worst cost of living crisis since the Great Depression. The NRL also received plenty of criticism from its own fans and pundits around the country, who criticised the announcement, the tax exemption being offered for new players, security issues, other teams missing out and sport mixing with politics. It is certain to be a hotly debated decision in the years ahead.

Whilst the NRL has supported the Pacific nations in recent years, most players are still Australian or New Zealand born, with most games being played in NZ or Australia, with the exception of PNG and some of Fiji's games, especially in 2024. Little has been done to improve the domestic leagues of some of the Pacific nations, with the exception of PNG, which has a team in the Queensland Cup and rapidly improving youth teams, pathways and systems, and Fiji, which now has a team the Kaiviti Silktails in the NSW Jersey Flegg, and has improved local leagues and pathway programmes for talented youth.

It is a top-down approach that is growing the game and supporter base but there are still major issues underneath this at the grassroots domestic level and the administration side for Pacific nations.

For myself and many fans from both hemispheres, it has been very disappointing that the NRL over such a long period of time has had no appetite for Ashes tours and the longer format tours, with the last real series way back in 2003 and the next one not until 2025, which is a shortened version played post-season after each competition's respective grand final, which does take a little of the gloss off the promotion and build-up of the series.

The Kangaroos brand has taken a huge hit, despite winning the last three World Cups, with too much inactivity and most games played deep into the off-season, well after the NRL Grand Final, which hurts growing the Kangaroos' brand and profile.

Many younger or newer fans today know little about the Green and Gold or the incredible history of the Kangaroos, where some of the sport's finest moments have occurred in that famous jersey, despite many younger fans thinking Origin is now the pinnacle of the game.

Both the Australian Kangaroos and the Great Britain Lions have played a huge role since 1908 in making rugby league what it is today, and that should never be forgotten.

Some of Australian sports' finest moments have come in the Kangaroo's jersey, with many famous victories over the years. One only has to look at the legendary names who have worn that famous jersey. Such names include Clive Churchill, Keith Holman, Ken Irvine, Johnny Raper, Reg Gasnier, Graeme Langlands, Arthur Beetson, Bob Fulton, Wally Lewis, Mal Meninga, Andrew Johns, Brad Fittler, Darren Lockyer, Johnathan Thurston, Cameron Smith, and many more.

Many fans and commentators still consider Game 2 of the 1990 Ashes series at Manchester's Old Trafford to be the greatest rugby league game of all time, with Australia pulling off a miracle to secure victory in the dying seconds of the match. Halfback Ricky Stuart broke through the British defence from deep inside his own half to find captain Mal Meninga in support, who barged and pushed defenders aside to seal an incredible victory, with television commentator David Morrow shouting in disbelief, *"Oh, what a try! What a try!!"* It still ranks as one of Australian sports' most iconic and greatest moments and will forever be etched in both our national history and Ashes folklore.

Many players today who are actually born in Australia or New Zealand are, in fact, preferring to align themselves with Pacific nations to honour family bloodlines, rather than play for the Kangaroos or New Zealand, despite being born and raised in these nations.

At best, the Kangaroos may play a maximum of three games a year in Australia, which is far too few if they wish to rebrand and rebuild the national team for supporters across the country.

The national team for any sport is always the best way to attract casual viewers to the sport. This has been seen with the nation jumping on the national team's success across multiple sports in major global events, such as the Wallabies, Socceroos and Matildas, and the national cricket team.

The Wallabies, Socceroos, and Matildas have all surpassed the Kangaroos in terms of popularity and brand profile, and this all comes down to the inactivity of the Kangaroos, not honouring the game's long-held traditions and history and allowing other sports to make major inroads, as well as the stronger international competition in other codes, with both rugby union and soccer having tremendous international competition that continues to expand and grow around the world. Rugby union is seeing tremendous growth in countries such as Japan and Argentina, which are now pushing and beating the top-tier nations in world rugby. Soccer is known as the world game and is unparalleled in its reach and popularity around the world.

The Matildas broke television records during the World Cup in 2023 that Australia hosted, with the semi-final game against England reaching an incredible 11.15 million viewers, the most watched programme in television history for Australia.

The international game is one layer in which the AFL does not have global competition or a competitive edge, and the NRL should have used this leverage to grow the game much more and make it a key strategy to fight back against the southern giant, which continues with its long strategic march into the northern states of New South Wales and Queensland.

The NRL will applaud itself and the media on its own website for its work in reviving the international game in recent years, but organising a Pacific Cup and Pacific Bowl deep into the post-season, with many of the players utilising the grandparent rule to play, will continue to receive criticism and cause confusion across the game when players are now playing Origin and then playing for a Pacific country, with some switching numerous times between countries. This is not going to take the game to the heights and potential it deserves, despite many supporting these rules to grow the sport.

The NRL is now slowly learning the importance of the international game and its incredible reach, but huge opportunities have been missed since the Super League war, and they now find themselves in a much more competitive and saturated international market to continue the long and proud history of the Kangaroos and raise the profile of the national team and win back the hearts and minds of the public.

Any revival of the national team profile must coincide with a return of the most important rivalry in the game: the Ashes, be it England or Great Britain against the

Kangaroos in a three-game series. This honours the game's long and proud history and is key to the future success for both leagues and countries and the greater health of the international game.

Both countries need each other more than they know or acknowledge, and the game as a whole needs a renaissance of this great rivalry to support the whole game with funding, sponsorships, television and media deals and more interest flowing off such a quality competition going head to head, which will support all nations that play rugby league.

Australia's arrogance towards not supporting the Ashes rivalry has hurt the game significantly and allowed other sports to win the hearts and minds of many supporters. The announcement of the return of the Ashes in 2025 is a major step in the right direction, with the upcoming series likely to receive enormous attention if England performs strongly. This would provide huge momentum for future series and be a great reminder of what the game has missed and what it has in its arsenal.

While the focus from the NRL has been on the regular league season and State of Origin in recent times, I have a funny feeling the upcoming Ashes series in late 2025 will be a harsh but healthy reminder of what they and the fans have missed out on and just how much potential it really has for the game and it, and not State of Origin, may be the jewel in the crown for the sport.

The 2017 World Cup final between Australia and England was one of the great modern games of rugby league, and fans should expect no less for the 2025 Ashes series as the anticipation begins to build. Let's hope Australian leaders and key stakeholders of the game get a dose of some real humility and gain an awareness and understanding of the vital importance of the Ashes for rugby league and everything it celebrates about the game and why it will always be the greatest rivalry in the sport.

THE FANS' GROWING APPETITE

ONE OF THE basic foundational laws of economics is the law of supply and demand. If leaders of the sport are reading the room correctly, there are clear signs, alongside strong empirical evidence to back this up, in the growing support, demand and interest for the international game that should be acted upon immediately and further supporting what this book is all about, with the renewal of the grandest and oldest international rivalry between England/Great Britain and Australia, which is still the pinnacle for many fans.

England played Samoa at home in October and November of 2024, with the two-game series seeing strong crowds in the north of England, with over 15,000 attending the first test match at Wigan and 16,000 attending in Leeds for the last match of the series. Whilst not huge numbers, these are solid figures when considering Samoa have nowhere near the profile of other major nations and have little away fan support in the UK. They were missing a number of high-profile players for the tour, plus the tour was sadly not confirmed until very late in the season, not allowing much time for more publicity and marketing. The UK is also facing some of the worst economic conditions since the Great Depression, with the cost of living affecting millions in the country including many rugby league and casual sporting supporters in the north, the heartland of the game in the UK.

The numbers were an improvement on the three-game series against Tonga in 2023, which attracted a total of just under 40,000 attending the series, which England won 3-0.

What was more impressive were the television figures on the BBC, with excellent figures across the two-game Samoan series, with a peak audience of 682,000 and an average of 513,000 for Game 1 of the series.

Game 2 ratings were even better, with a peak audience of 844,000 and an average of 741,000, which further supports the belief of the growing interest and demand for the international game from fans and casual viewers in the UK.

To put this into perspective, the 2024 Super League Grand Final at Old Trafford between Wigan and Hull KR, screened on pay television provider Sky Sports, attracted an average audience of 373,000.

These are telling numbers and outline both the importance of free-to-air television for the code and the importance of the international game to attract a wider fan base to the sport. Can you imagine what those numbers will be when Australia play England in the 2025 Ashes series? We should expect and hope to see well over a million viewers for each game, which is just fabulous for the sport as a whole and will lead to more interest in the code, more fans, plus more articles, podcasts and media attention, which leads to more sponsorship and more money for the code.

The 2024 Pacific nations tournament in the southern hemisphere played between Australia, New Zealand and Tonga also saw excellent attendances across the tournament, with a tournament high of 33,196 attending the opener at Brisbane between Tonga and Australia. The match between the Kiwis and the Kangaroos a week later at Christchurch sold out, with 17,000 in attendance. The next weekend, over 22,000 fans watched Tonga play arch rivals New Zealand in Auckland, and the final between Australia and Tonga played at Bankwest Stadium in Sydney was sold out, with nearly 29,000 attending the final. A sea of red dominated the crowd in support of Tonga, with Australia dominating the match with a 20-14 victory.

The free-to-air television ratings in Australia were also very encouraging and were far stronger than many NRL club games and higher than rugby union's showpiece, the Bledisloe Cup, which again outlines the growing interest and support for international rugby league.

It was reported a number of the games across all media platforms passed the one million figure, which is fantastic news for the sport.

Free-to-air numbers only below:

- Australia vs Tonga - 698k - excluding Fox/Kayo

- Australia vs New Zealand - 586k - excluding Fox/Kayo
- New Zealand vs Tonga - 546k - excluding Fox/Kayo
- Australia vs Tonga - 614k - excluding Fox/Kayo

When you add in Foxtel and Kayo pay television numbers in Australia, plus the New Zealand and Tonga figures, the numbers are very promising for the sport, and show the keen appetite for high-quality international rugby league that is slowly seeing a revival after many years of inactivity and meaningless fixtures.

Outside strong ticket sales and healthy television ratings, the tournament also saw strong merchandise sales, with jerseys and other merchandise all in high demand.

Tonga's fans deserve much praise for their part in the revival of international rugby league and their absolute dedication to support their national team, with games in Brisbane, Auckland and Sydney seeing more support for Tonga than home team nations.

The only downside is that Tonga seems to not be commercially viable at this point in time to play home fixtures in Tonga, with the country's total population of just 105,000, where facilities and commercial arrangements do not seem to be economically viable or attractive at this time. They are likely to continue to play home fixtures in New Zealand or Australia.

This is one area rugby league must improve on, as most nations which play international rugby union can now play

The Fans' Growing Appetite

games and series at home venues, where they are also commercially viable, which has added considerable depth, interest and expansion to the international game. We have seen significant improvement in nations such as Japan and Argentina in recent years, with Japan hosting the 2019 World Cup and Argentina now one of the strongest teams in world rugby. I was very surprised to learn of the growth and popularity of rugby union in Portugal when I visited the country in early 2024, with the national team having strong growth in a soccer dominated country, with merchandise regularly available in most major sporting stores. Many newer countries to the game around the world are also seeing significant growth in the game, like Portugal and Georgia, and many countries across Africa, South America, North America and Europe. This is all off the back of regular and meaningful international competition, and especially if they have performed well in the World Cup.

Papua New Guinea has made tremendous progress in rugby league, with home fixtures now played at Port Moresby, where they have a quality stadium and sound investment and commercial arrangements. Fiji has also hosted international games in recent years, and will look to further its presence as an island nation in years to come.

Outside of the strong television ratings and attendances to cap off the 2024 season for both the southern and northern hemispheres, I have long believed that there is strong appetite for more international rugby league from fans that is just waiting to be tapped, and that leaders of the sport have not read the room well and planned accordingly to cater for this growing demand.

In simple terms, fans of all countries want more international rugby league. You see this in fans' forums on websites, discussing the future of the sport on podcasts, social media, the many fans who long for bygone eras of the sport, with regular internal competition, and especially when watching other sports that have tremendous success with their own international events, which make many fans envious.

The formula for success is not that hard: high-quality international rugby league played in meaningful series or tournaments, which is built upon year after year and is planned well in advance, with good promotion and coverage, to become a commercially viable and then profitable investment.

Fans want more international rugby league, and it makes sense when the regular season for both the NRL and Super League is now leaving little room for expanded international competition. They want to support the international game and support home nations and see the best against the best, just like other sports around the world, and they want more internationals and less club rugby league. The international game brings far more excitement than just another club fixture, especially in the UK, with the numerous loop fixtures across the season.

That leaves us with the growing appetite for Australia vs England in an Ashes series. As mentioned, the two giants of rugby league have not played against each other since the 2017 World Cup final, and many fans are now clamouring to see the old rivals face off once again.

The enormous interest in the upcoming Ashes series was confirmed when tickets went on sale to the general public in early April 2025, with two of the test matches being sold out immediately for the three-game series. The third test match at Headingley Leeds sold out in minutes, and the second test match at the new Everton stadium in Liverpool also sold out quickly. The first test will be hosted at Wembley, and organisers are hoping for a huge crowd, with many hopeful all three games can be sold out.

At the time of writing (August 2025), a reported 110,000 tickets have been sold for the 2025 Ashes Series.

To put this in perspective, the 2003 Ashes series had a total of 74,000 in attendance across the three-game series, and we are already past those figures for the 2025 series, even before a ball has been kicked or a tackle made.

My only criticism is playing the third test at Headingley Leeds, which has a capacity of only 20,000. I understand the promoters' and organisers' theory of selling this game out to create more demand for Wembley and Everton, but I believe there was strong enough interest in the series to be played in three large stadiums across the UK.

English fans now have a team with emerging talent which has performed strongly against Tonga and Samoa in the last 2 years, and fans and players now all want to know if England can beat Australia and break the long hoodoo that has lasted since 1970 in an Ashes series and 1972 in a major title involving Australia.

So many questions are waiting to be answered for the upcoming 2025 Ashes series. Just how good is England and can they compete with the Kangaroos? Is Australia still the dominant force of world rugby league or are they in decline?

Just how good are certain players from both teams and can they handle the stress and pressure of an Ashes series environment? Just how passionate are the fans for the Ashes? What size crowd attendance will we see for Wembley? Will the media buy into the series and provide plenty of coverage across the numerous outlets? What will the television figures for the series be? There are so many questions that will be answered as anticipation grows for the first Ashes series in many years.

You can tell that English coach Shaun Wane and his players are itching to play Australia and that this upcoming series means a lot to the English, who have now had such a long wait to face the Kangaroos. Australia's decision to swap the series to be played in England instead of Australia, with the full support of then coach Mal Meninga and the NRL, provides a clear signal of the Aussies' desire to play the Poms and experience what Meninga did over his long career with a record four Kangaroo tours, still a record for any Australian player.

Make no mistake: there is great anticipation for the upcoming 2025 Ashes series from both fans and players, and this will probably be the best build-up to any international series since the 2017 World Cup final. I expect this momentum to really build as the series gets closer and more marketing and promotions are seen for the three-game series.

The 2025 Ashes series has all the makings of a new and exciting chapter in the greatest rivalry in rugby league, and one rugby league must build on and make the most of to ensure its legacy and future for many years to come.

TOURS - THE WOW EVENT FACTOR

I MUST ADMIT, I have always had a certain degree of envy for what international rugby union has to offer with major events for fans, with World Cups that now move around the world, and hosts of the event now coming from from all corners of the world, from New Zealand (2011), England (2015), Japan (2019), France (2023), Australia (2027), to British and Irish Lions tours every 4 years to either Australia, New Zealand or South Africa, Six-Nations tournaments, Bledisloe Cups, the Four-Nations Rugby Championship, and the rivalry that just gets better and better between New Zealand and South Africa, which has become Origin-like in recent times.

Rugby's ambition to expand the game globally is taking an even further step, with the USA to host the men's 2031 Rugby World Cup as the code looks to make strong inroads into the North American sporting market after building a strong foundation in the domestic market in both Canada and America.

Despite its struggles at the domestic level in many countries, the sport continues to see massive growth across Africa, South America, Europe, North America and many other countries around the world.

Whilst rugby union may have many challenges at the lower levels with finances for professional club rugby union and the decline of the community game level in some countries, one thing they do extremely well is create events around the international game that have the wow factor that excites fans from around the world, often many years in advance, and is a major driver of the growing interest in the sport around the world.

The wow event factor is critical to any sport's success and is one that rugby league needs to become acutely aware of, as every sport has and needs to be in an ultra competitive sporting and entertainment market. The Superbowl, World Series Baseball, NBA Finals, FA Cup Final, UEFA Champions League Final, Summer and Winter Olympics, Tour De France, The Masters, Ashes Cricket, World Cups across many different sports including soccer, rugby union and cricket, Wimbledon and the other major grand slams in tennis, the Bathurst car race, the Boxing Day test at the MCG are just a few examples of major sporting events that are looked upon each calendar year and in some cases many years ahead with excitement and anticipation from fans of their respective sports or casual sport lovers.

When you look at the calendar for rugby league each

season, games with the wow event factor are quite small compared to rugby union's impressive international schedule.

For the NRL in Australia/New Zealand, I would say each season has only a few really big wow events that bring excitement to any season and attract more casual fans, these being:

- State of Origin
- NRL Grand Final
- NRL preliminary finals, which have now become major events in their own right before the grand finals
- Magic Round - while not my cup of tea, the event has sold out in recent years and is looked upon eagerly for each new season by many fans, who converge on Brisbane for 3-4 days in a festival-like environment.

The UK has even fewer wow event factor events each calendar year, with just three major events after promotion and relegation now being removed for a licence model for Super League:

- Challenge Cup Final
- Magic Round
- Super League Grand Final

I would also have included the World Club Challenge as a major event for the game in both hemispheres, but this is hard to include in the list above when the event was cancelled for 2025 and no date has been locked in for 2026 and may yet again clash with Las Vegas. I personally believe this game is a huge event on the rugby league calendar that should be promoted and treated as such to align with its importance and value to the sport as a major event that has enormous untapped potential.

The one glaring gap for both leagues is the lack of major events for international rugby league. Whilst any internationals are great, just adding them to the end of season will not ensure they become wow events that capture a wider audience, especially when played in Australia as the weather becomes hotter and cricket season commences, and when many fans by then have footy fatigue.

Once upon a time for the Australian public and for most players, the Kangaroo tour to the UK was the pinnacle of the game, a major event that only came along once every 4 years, which made it more prestigious and anticipated by both players and fans. The excitement of the upcoming tour grows as the date gets closer, across both the Origin series and the NRL regular season, as to which players would be selected for the tour and how the team would perform compared to past tours and whether they could win the Ashes against the Poms.

The last four extended Kangaroo tours to the UK will forever live in the folklore of rugby league. The 1982 and 1986 Invincibles tours, and then the 1990 and 1994 tours led by captain and now former Australian coach Mal Meninga, were all memorable tours and the last of their kind for the sport.

What made those tours unique and greatly anticipated by

both Australian and British fans? History was being honoured, tradition, hatred from both nations, Britain's long drought, scarcity with the away tours only being every 4 years, club games as part of the tour, which built momentum and excitement for the tests, three major tests, famous football stadiums, extended playing squads with both A and B teams, extended tours that not only included club games but also games against the Welsh and French to spread the rugby league gospel, all added up to make the tours such a highlight for the code.

The last extended conventional Kangaroo tour to the UK was way back in 1994, when 28 players were selected for the tour and 18 games were played on the tour, with a total attendance of 269,277 across the tour, compared to more recent Ashes tours in 2001 and 2003, when only three and six games were played respectively, as the tours were jammed into tighter schedules. Australia has toured since 2003, but these have been in competitions that are based on tri and quad nation formats rather than head-to-head tours like the Ashes that can also include many touring games on the schedule.

The 1982 and 1986 Kangaroo tours to the UK played 22 and 20 games respectively.

This was the 18-game tour itinerary for the 1994 Kangaroo tour that ran from October to December, with the three tests against Great Britain the highlight of the tour:

- Cumbria
- Leeds
- Wigan

- Castleford
- Halifax
- **Great Britain - 1st test**
- Sheffield
- Wales
- St Helens
- **Great Britain - 2nd test**
- Warrington
- Bradford Northern
- Great Britain U21s
- **Great Britain - 3rd test**
- French Presidents Xlll
- Roussillon/Catalan XIII
- French Xlll
- France

Talk to any ex-Kangaroo player and they all say the tours were a magnificent experience and often the highlight of their playing career, where it went beyond just rugby. Many great friendships were made on tours, and the players got to experience travelling and playing across the UK and France. It was a trip of a lifetime, playing across the United Kingdom in front of the British fans, creating memories that will last forever, with players away for over 2 months.

In modern professional sport, with many games being jammed into an already tight schedule, the extended tour is becoming more and more rare for not only rugby league but any sport outside of cricket, as professional leagues dictate the schedule and finances of most sports.

The 1994 Kangaroos tour to the UK with 18 games played, including games against many UK club teams, plus games in Wales and France, seems incredible to many newer or younger fans to the sport today. Many are only used to the structured NRL or Super League season we now see that is dictated by television and media companies, with often only a few rep games at the end of the season, if any. As mentioned in an earlier chapter, both the NRL clubs and NRL head office have been some of the biggest blockers of international rugby league and extended Ashes tours with club games.

1992 was the last conventional Great Britain Lions tour Down Under, which included 17 games, with six test matches against Papua New Guinea, Australia and New Zealand, plus games against NRL clubs and lower level rep teams from New South Wales and Queensland and other New Zealand and Papua New Guinea teams. The tour was jammed into 6 weeks, running from May until July, with State of Origin played before the Ashes series.

This was the tour itinerary from the 1992 British Lions tour to Papua New Guinea, Australia and New Zealand:

- Highland Zone PNG

- Island Zone PNG
- Papua New Guinea test
- Queensland Residents
- Canberra Raiders
- Illawarra Steelers
- **Australia - 1st test**
- NSW Country Firsts
- Parramatta
- Newcastle
- **Australia - 2nd test**
- Gold Coast
- **Australia - 3rd test**
- Auckland (NZ)
- New Zealand 1st test
- Canterbury (NZ)
- New Zealand 2nd test

The British and Irish Lions rugby union team is one of the most famous names in world sport and one of the few international teams that still tours. Every 4 years, the Lions, in their famous red jersey, will tour either Australia, New Zealand or South Africa, with each taking their turn to host the Lions, made up of the best players in the UK and Ireland. It is one of the highlights of any calendar year when the Lions tour. Such is the scarcity of the tours, that host nations only host the lions once every 12 years, with Australia hosting their last tours in 2001 and 2013.

2025 will be the next tour for the British Lions, who will tour Australia after an incredible tour of New Zealand in 2017, which captured the imagination of the world's sporting public with the three-game series drawn in what many fans believe was one of the greatest series of all time. The Lions toured South Africa in 2021, with the series being won by South Africa two games to one in another tight contest that was severely affected by COVID.

The Lions will play nine games on their 6-week 2025 Australian tour, with the schedule as follows:

- June 28 vs Western Force, Perth
- July 2 vs Queensland Reds, Brisbane
- July 5 vs NSW Waratahs, Sydney
- July 9 vs ACT Brumbies, Canberra
- July 12 vs Invitational AUS and NZ, Adelaide
- **July 19 vs Wallabies (1st test), Brisbane**
- July 22 vs First Nations & Pasifika XV, Melbourne
- **July 26 vs Wallabies (2nd test), Melbourne**
- **August 2 vs Wallabies (3rd test), Sydney**

The highlight of the tour is the three tests against the Wallabies, with games shared across Brisbane, Melbourne and Sydney, with other tour games against Australian Super Rugby club teams in the Western Force, Queensland Reds, New South Wales Waratahs and the Australian Capital Territory (ACT) Brumbies, a game against the First Nations and Pasifika XV in Melbourne, plus an invitational game in Adelaide made up of Australian and New Zealand players, which many fans are already labelling the unofficial fourth test of the tour.

The tour is certain to attract massive international attention, with games being held across the country in all major capital cities, and is the biggest sporting event in Australia for 2025, with over 500k tickets already sold, with the last Lions tour being held 12 years ago, back in 2013. Ticket sales have been strong and large crowd attendances are expected for all of the games as the anticipation for the tour grows and promotion and publicity really kick in as excitement builds. Rugby Australia announced they are expecting over 40,000 UK and Irish fans to travel to Australia for the tour, with around 100,000 fans likely to attend the second test match at Melbourne's hallowed MCG. Test matches in Sydney and Brisbane are expected to sell out, as the tour creates enormous interest both at home and abroad.

If ever rugby league needed a wake-up call to outline the importance of the Ashes series and international rugby league, this upcoming Lions tour to Australia will be that wake-up call to rugby league officials in both the southern and northern hemisphere about what the code is missing out on.

Tours - The Wow Event Factor

The 2025 Lions tour will be an absolute monster for rugby, with hundreds of thousands of fans to attend matches. The television ratings will be enormous, both at home and abroad, especially if the series is close. Merchandise sales will be massive, and the impact on the Australian economy will be huge, as motels, hotels, pubs, bars, restaurants and tourist attractions all benefit from the large numbers of tourists from the UK and Ireland, and Rugby Australia receives big support from state and federal government in hosting the Lions.

Most of all, the tour will make rugby cool and popular again, which will flow from the top of the code to grassroots levels and bring plenty of optimism, ambition and possibilities to the sport once again, especially after some very tough and dark years for the sport in Australia. It could be given further momentum when Australia hosts the 2027 Rugby Union World Cup, which could lead to both events kickstarting a revival and renaissance for the code in Australia.

Both the Lions and Rugby Australia will receive a financial windfall from the tour in the tens of millions, which will help both the Australians and the Lions, after many tough years for both domestic leagues since COVID. It is reported the Australian Rugby Union is set to pocket $100 million plus for the tour, which is a godsend for the code after many tough years when the code looked down and out for good, lost its contract or did not renew its contract with Fox Sports and was unable to find any financial backers. The game was virtually on life support in Australia.

The numbers don't lie, and rugby league officials from both hemispheres should take a strong interest in them. The last British and Irish Lions tour to Australia in 2013 granted a surplus of $35 million more for Australian Rugby Union than would normally be expected for a regular home series. $150 million was bought into the Australian economy, with over 30,000 visitors for the tour, and allowed the then cash-strapped ARU to make a $19.5 million profit for the 2013 season. That is the power and leverage of major events and what that can do for any sport, especially in the international format. I am sure the British rugby league would kill for that cash injection at the moment, after a decade of media revenues falling, much like what the Wallabies have been through in Australia.

The Lions tour to New Zealand in 2017 did similar numbers for New Zealand rugby, with NZR making a huge $33.4 million profit for that financial year.

The financial windfall from the British and Irish Lions 10-match tour was the driving force behind a record $224 million private investment deal for the national game, NZR said in a press release after the series.

The profit from the tour saved New Zealand rugby in many ways, with the 2017 profit being $33.4m compared against a loss of $7m in 2016. That is the power of international rugby and wow events.

Even with COVID allowing no spectators to attend or tour for the South African vs Lions series in 2021 in South Africa, the British Lions still made a profit of £8.2 million (€9.6m). It was reported SA Rugby would have had to close its doors if it were not for the British and Irish Lions tour.

Despite no fans or tourists being in attendance, the South

African Union was able to break even in 2021 after 12 months of pandemic chaos. SA Rugby reported a modest profit of 9 million rand (£450k) for 2021, all off the back of the Lions tour. Jurie Roux, CEO of SA Rugby, said at the time that if it were not for the visit of the Lions, which at one point looked set to be scrapped, the union would have not have been able to keep its doors open.

Many rugby league fans forget that the Great Britain Lions, like their rugby union counterparts, were once one of the major drawcards and wow factors for the game. Who can ever forget the Lions' famous victory on the last traditional Ashes tour Down Under in 1992, when Great Britain stunned the Kangaroos with a 33-10 win at Melbourne's Princes Park! With an estimated 10,000 Brits in attendance, this still ranks as one of the Lions' last great victories against Australia.

If rugby league wants to keep up with its rugby union counterparts and create its own excitement with the international game, then a rebirth of the Ashes and conventional longer tours is a must.

While 18-game tours to the UK may not be feasible with the length of the regular season for both the NRL and Super League, tours that can capture the public attention and interest and have those wow factor events can be created and designed into any yearly calendar.

Even if the Kangaroos returned to more traditional tours and only played 8-10 games like the Lions rugby union tour to Australia in 2025, these tours would still create enormous publicity and interest for the game and build anticipation for the Ashes series.

Here is a rough tour guide for a possible future Kangaroos tour that reverts back to the more conventional and traditional format like the 1994 tour played on a smaller scale:

Game 1 vs Leeds

Game 2 vs Wigan

Game 3 vs Great Britain 1st test (London)

Game 4 vs St Helens

Game 5 vs Wales

Game 6 vs Great Britain 2nd test (Newcastle)

Game 7 vs Hull KR or Hull FC

Game 8 vs Great Britain 3rd test (Manchester)

Game 9 vs France

This draft itinerary is still a great tour that includes big club games against some of Super League's strongest clubs, which would have many fans excited, growth games in both Wales and France to spread the game and to grow the Kangaroos' brand internationally, like the All Blacks, Springboks or Irish have done in recent years, with the highlight of the tour the Ashes series, held over three games across both the north and south of England in big stadiums.

Let's reverse the tour, with Great Britain or England touring Australia:

Game 1 vs Newcastle

Game 2 vs Parramatta

Game 3 vs Australia 1st test (Sydney)

Game 4 vs Brisbane/Dolphins

Game 5 vs North Queensland/Gold Coast

Game 6 vs Australia 2nd test (Brisbane)

Game 7 vs Melbourne

Game 8 vs Australia 3rd test (Melbourne)

Game 9 vs PNG

Game 10 vs NZ

Again, these are big club games that would have plenty of interest for both television and for attracting fans attending games, tests against PNG and NZ or other Pacific nations could be added, plus the big three tests against Australia in major stadiums across Sydney, Brisbane and Melbourne.

If the NRL clubs did not want to play the English, then alternatives could include WA, NSW Country, or QLD Country fixtures, but if the Great Britain Lions or England can have a revival and build a stong playing group with plenty of depth and talent, it would be financial suicide for NRL clubs to miss an opportunity to play the Great Britain Lions or English touring team, which would be a financial windfall for clubs and the greater game.

The NRL clubs have been some of the biggest blockers of the international game, worried that star players may get injured or they will lose out financially with fewer club games, but the exact opposite view is taken by Super Rugby clubs in both Australia and New Zealand. They all want nothing more than the opportunity and privilege to be able to play the touring Lions. They know the importance and benefit for both their own clubs and the greater game, with a massive financial windfall across the tour in gate tickets and merchandise, bigger crowds than for most club games, brand growth to a bigger and wider audience, including international audiences, and keeping tradition with the past tours and growing the game.

If Great Britain or England can become as good as I believe they can and not only compete with Australia but defeat or really push Australia, then I can assure you, NRL club teams will be lining up to want to play Great Britain or England in the longer format tours, as we see now for both the Lions tours to New Zealand in 2017 and Australia in 2025. It would be an honour and privilege for any club to be selected to host the touring Lions team, and the windfall of the game would spread across the whole game, like we are seeing with Lions rugby union tours to southern hemisphere nations.

There is a glaring omission of big events for the international game on the rugby league calendar outside the World Cup, which, to be honest, has yet to capture the hearts and minds of the international sporting public. The Ashes is a no-brainer for both southern and northern hemisphere tours.

Rugby Australia is going to get a lot of momentum and attention from the 2025 British and Irish Lions tour, and in many ways, the success of the tour will leave many clues for what rugby league should do with rekindling its very own Ashes tours in the longer traditional format that includes club and international games, both at home and in the UK.

Rugby league needs more wow events for the code, and the revival and renaissance of the Ashes tour is one that makes all the sense in the world and ticks all the boxes both strategically and commercially, and fulfills the desires of fans, players and many clubs.

SCHEDULING

IF THERE IS one thing that rugby league does awfully badly, it is in the planning and scheduling for the international game, both short and long term.

In reality, the game has no real long-term fixed schedule, despite public relations statements from the IRL, the NRL and the RFL. It chops and changes its own schedule each year, often scheduling tours or series with far less than a year's notice. Sometimes it is even shorter notice, as seen with England not knowing if Samoa would tour there in 2024 until only a few months before the first test match, and, despite a few events locked in the schedule, has no real long-term scheduled itinerary outside of the World Cup. The World Cup has had its own flaws, with both France and America unable to find the financial guarantees to host the 2025 RLWC, with the event now to be hosted in 2026 across Australia and Papua New Guinea.

The 2025 World Club Challenge was a perfect example of

Scheduling

the code's poor scheduling, which would have seen four-time champion NRL premiers, the Penrith Panthers, take on the all-conquering Wigan Warriors team in what would have been a mouthwatering blockbuster rematch of the 2024 World Club Challenge. Sadly, for fans, this was unable to be played, due to both teams playing in Las Vegas in March to kickstart the 2025 season, and, with little free time available to reschedule, the game was thus cancelled. This was a huge opportunity missed for the game in what would have been one of the highlights of the season and which would have attracted enormous attention from both English and Australian fans. It was one of the few games and events that had that wow factor and which would have attracted many casual viewers, especially after the classic contest in 2024 with Wigan upsetting Penrith 16-12 in a nailbiter in front of a full house at Wigan. What a terrible failure from the sports leaders for not making the World Club Challenge a priority for the 2025 schedule and ensuring it was locked into the schedule before Las Vegas, and then having no backup plan to reschedule the game if teams locked in to play in Las Vegas won the 2024 grand final. Again, it seemed the NRL and Penrith had less appetite to play the game on a new date, with Wigan CEO Kris Radlinski doing a media tour after Wigan's 2024 grand final victory over Hull KR, urging the game to be played despite the Las Vegas scheduling clash, even at the Magic Round in Brisbane, if possible, with Penrith having the bye for the Magic Round in Brisbane. But unfortunately, this was unable to be confirmed or rearranged, and so the code and fans missed out on one of the great games and major events of the rugby league season.

A structured, consistent and well planned long-term

schedule is key to any sports success. Cricket has a long-term schedule with World Cups, T20 World Cups, and test matches, and both Australia and England fans know years in advance when the Ashes will be played, both at home and abroad. Rugby union's international schedule is well planned, with World Cup hosts announced many years in advance, and major tours like the British and Irish Lions to Australia in 2025 are planned well in advance, which gives the fans plenty of time to plan and organise tickets and enjoy holidays.

Look at tennis and golf, which are both major international sports and which each have four major grand slams each year as the highlights of each calendar season, plus an itinerary with many other events around the world.

The UFC has been able to overtake boxing in America in terms of popularity and commercial numbers, and this all stems from consistent cards and fights across the calendar year, with one event finishing, and then planning immediately beginning for future events, with fight cards all on its website. This creates ongoing momentum for the sport. The UFC also ensures the best against the best, with no easy matchups for champion fighters. This will always sell in any sport, when it's the best against the best in elite head-to-head competition.

If the Ashes is to recapture its place as one of the pinnacles of the game, it has to become entrenched on the rugby league calendar and scheduled both for 2025 and many years ahead. Whilst it was great news when it was announced that Australia would tour the UK in late 2025 for the first Ashes series in many years, one must not forget that in the original announcement, the English were going to tour Down Under for the Ashes, but this was later reversed in late 2024 when it was announced Australia instead would tour the UK. You could not imagine this major switch occurring in other major sports such as cricket or rugby union, especially when some fans had started buying tickets and planning trips to Australia. Rugby union and cricket, as mentioned, have locked in long-term schedules and do not leave things to the last minute or switch tours. Tours are often announced many years in advance, giving fans plenty of notice and time to prepare for the tours and time to promote these events. That level of professionalism and commitment is badly needed for the revival of the Ashes and international rugby league.

The biggest obstacles to the revival of the Ashes, longer tours and a stronger international programme is the length of both the NRL and Super League seasons. The NRL season commences with trials in early February and concludes with the NRL Grand Final on the October long weekend, with the Super League season going even longer. Trials start on Boxing Day with the annual Leeds vs Wakefield game, and the season concludes about 1- 2 weeks after the NRL Grand Final with the grand final showpiece at Old Trafford.

The only way the game can revive the Ashes and international rugby league and keep up with international rugby union, which is growing very fast around the world and in many new growth markets, is for both the NRL and Super League to cut the regular season games and allocate time for high-quality international rugby league, with the Ashes at the core of this strategy. Both the NRL and Super League had 27 rounds across the regular season for 2024, excluding finals, and the UK also had the Challenge Cup competition, with the NRL playing 24 games in the regular season and the Super League playing 27 rounds with no byes.

The Super League are playing so many games across both competitions, which includes endless loop fixtures now with only 12 teams in the league, to the anger of many fans, with the clubs and owners wanting this for more revenue, but it dilutes and devalues the product when clubs are facing each other three or four times a season. Investing in a stronger international programme with the Ashes as the centrepiece outside the World Cup would be wise for all parties, who look to add a new layer of revenue for the sport that could far eclipse what many in the game believe is possible. Why could the Ashes not make the kind of revenue that Origin is currently making in Australia or the 2025 British and Irish Lions tour is for rugby union or the money that is coming in for the Ashes cricket series?

Between 1990 and 1994, 10 games were played between Great Britain and Australia, nine in the Ashes series and one at the 1992 rugby league World Cup Final at Wembley. Those games were played in front of capacity crowds in major stadiums including Wembley London, Lang Park Brisbane, Sydney Football Stadium, Elland Road Leeds and Old Trafford at Manchester. So we have been at the mountain before and the code can definitely reach the mountain again and have big tours and big games in big stadiums that create even greater publicity, awareness and interest. Many in the game have somehow forgotten this and need to be reminded, especially when we see the British and Irish Lions rugby tour Down

Scheduling

Under in 2025 receive enormous interest and publicity and see the test series played in front of packed stadiums.

Whilst I do personally think the Las Vegas NRL season opener is a mixture of good and bad for the game, I still have concerns that the major purpose for the event and promotion is the NRL trying to gain a foothold in the huge American gambling market, rather than really trying to grow the sport organically in America with a sound foundation at the base level. One good thing to come out of it for the 2025 event is the collaboration between the NRL and Super League, with the invitation to include both Wigan and Warrington in the 2025 event schedule, plus the English women's rugby league team, who took on the Australian Jillaroos. It makes sense and is good business for all parties, and is good leverage from what we have to offer. The English teams boosted ticket sales and interest for Las Vegas, with a reported 10,000 making the trip across the Atlantic for the event from the UK. It is a sure bet to boost ratings, attendance and interest in the season opener and add great value to the event.

The 2026 Las Vegas event has already seen strong ticket sales from the UK, with Leeds and Hull KR the British representatives for 2026.

A collaborative and supportive relationship between the NRL and Super League/RFL is a must to re-establish the Ashes and longer-format tours in both hemispheres and grow the sport in both hemispheres.

Key factors that are currently impacting the scheduling of the Ashes and more international rugby are:

- Too many club games each year in both the NRL and Super League

- Length of season leaving little space on the calendar for international rugby league

- No designated rep schedule or itinerary for the Ashes and the international game

- Insufficient funding to really commit to international rugby league

- NRL and Super League clubs not supporting international rugby league

- Too many amendments and changes to the international schedule, making the code look less professional than other sports.

The funding matter is vital, with the NRL and its clubs in a much stronger position compared to its Super League counterparts. The key difference is the television money, with the NRL's current media deal dwarfing Super League's current deals. Whilst they are going in totally different directions in terms of media deals and the amount of money for each league, there should be key alignment from both leagues and the huge benefits for both parties in the revival of the Ashes and longer-format tours. The NRL leaders have recently openly said they want to play fewer fixtures moving forward. With media deals growing each year, they are in a position to make this a reality and also to grow the international game in the process, with fewer club games. Super League is playing more and more games and unnecessary loop fixtures, often out of the necessity for more money, with television deals from Sky Sports declining in recent years and many clubs struggling. The Ashes and the international game can offer huge benefits to English Super League clubs and the greater British game, and could spark a renaissance for the game, with more interest and potentially more money flowing off the back of the international game, as seen with many rugby union and cricket countries, where the national team drives the profile and finances for the whole sport.

Both league governing bodies must enforce and ensure all NRL and Super League clubs are fully behind the expansion and promotion of the Ashes and international rugby league. The Ashes can never become the pinnacle of the game if clubs continue to block it and never support it or not want star players to participate.

If the Ashes is to be revived, some key actions that must be taken immediately for the schedule are:

- Reduce both the NRL and Super League regular season. I think the NRL can go down to anywhere between 18-22 rounds with future media deals.

- The Super League is not as fortunate as its NRL counterpart financially, but any reduction will support the game and allow for more focus on the Ashes.

- A bare minimum option is to reduce the amount of regular season games in the years when the Ashes series are to be played.

Now, an all-important question: When should the Ashes be played?

Many fans believe there should be a representative break schedule, with some believing it should be played mid-year around June or July, and others thinking it should be at the completion of the NRL and Super League season.

I firmly believe that the format of future Ashes tours beyond 2025, both in the UK and Australia, should include touring sides playing club games and other internationals, alongside the three-match Ashes series.

For the Kangaroos touring the UK and France, I think we need to look backwards to go forwards, to those magnificent tours of 1982,1986, 1990 and 1994, which all happened at the end of the NRL season and were a huge success.

One of the benefits of a Kangaroos tour to the UK and France from, say, late October to early December, is that this aligns with the cooler winter months, contrary to Australia.

Future Kangaroos tours should run from mid to late October or early November until early December and keep the tradition of previous tours.

For future England/Great Britain Lions tours to Australia, I personally don't think at the end of the NRL and Super League season will work to its full potential, due to a number of factors, including footy fatigue, the cricket season commencing, which takes all the attention and publicity, and maybe the biggest issue is the summer months' heat, which makes attending, watching and playing rugby league impossible, especially in Queensland. Hot weather is not

Scheduling

conducive to attractive rugby league from both a player's and a fan's perspective.

That leaves no other alternative but for future English and Great Britain Lions tours to be played mid-season in Australia, like we saw for the last Great Britain Lions tour in 1992, and the same model for the British and Irish Lions rugby team, who will tour Australia from June to August in 2025.

This will upset many Super League and NRL clubs, as any tour Down Under would clash with the NRL and Super League. My response would be that a tour Down Under would only happen once every 4 years and that this is a priority for the sport. To lessen the effect of a tour Down Under, byes could be arranged for clubs, reduced season games for when an Ashes tour occurs, split rounds, or even putting some competitions on hold for 2-4 weeks to lessen the impact, or continuing with the competition in normal mode, with replacement players called on to cover for selected players. There is no easy fix, but the option of not playing the Ashes or more international rugby league would be dire for the sport. Its importance and strategic value to the code will be fully recognised when the British and Irish Lions tour in 2025 and when the end profit is announced for the tour.

These tours could be played anywhere between May and August, and it probably makes sense to hold them after the State of Origin series, so they would gain momentum and be a preselection for the Kangaroos team.

To plan, create and implement a proper Ashes tour and more international rugby league is not that hard, but self interest is pulling the game back, and sacrifice has to be made.

This has already hurt the international game considerably over the last two decades or more.

Cut the NRL and Super League games, lock in Ashes tours many years in advance, promote the hell out of them, and risk-manage scheduled club competitions clashes as best you can. It's not that difficult, but it takes real commitment and a vision, something rugby league leaders are not known for.

FINANCIAL SUSTAINABILITY

SOME OF THE harshest critics for the return of a proper Ashes series, extended tours and more international rugby league say the game can't afford to endorse and support more international rugby league in the face of fewer NRL or Super League games, as the game will lose money with fewer televised games, as this is the major source of revenue for the game outside of match attendances and other forms of sponsorship from major corporations, gambling and the government.

Some of these critics are NRL and Super League clubs and club owners who are often only worried about their own bottom line and personal interests and don't want to lose money for their clubs or the greater game to promote more international rugby league, and have only self interest at heart. There are some clubs and owners who see the bigger picture and are supportive of more international rugby league, but there are still many clubs and owners from both leagues involved who do not fully support the Ashes or more international rugby league on the yearly calendar at the expense of fewer NRL and Super League fixtures.

To put this to the test, imagine if Great Britain or England were touring Australia mid-year, how would clubs feel if the NRL and Super League/RFL leaders told clubs they would lose four to six games in revenue, their best players would be unavailable or may get injured, and there would be no reimbursement unless the tour made a profit? There would be cries of disapproval and outrage about such a decision!

I would argue the game has already lost a fortune over the last 20 years plus for not fully committing to international rugby league and not playing an Ashes series in over 20 years, and allowing rugby union and other sports to dominate the national team sporting profile and to expand their international games for their respective sports.

Not playing an Ashes series since 2003 may be one of, if not the worst, decisions in the code's history when you look at what has occurred for cricket and rugby union in the same period.

Many fans, myself included, find it incredibly sad that a proper Ashes series full tour has not been seen since 1994. It really is sad that the grand tradition of the game has been forgotten and forsaken for more club games.

While there's no doubt there is growing appetite for more international rugby league, with more work been done to grow the game in the Pacific in recent years, and anticipation growing fast for the first Ashes series in many years in late 2025, for the long-term stability and ensured future of the Ashes and international rugby league, the finances need to be sustainable and built on sound foundations to ensure longevity of the Ashes series post 2025 and to also push back against critics of the upcoming and future series who will look for their own best interest over the greater game's wellbeing.

The number one criterion is to ensure the Ashes series is a financial success and provides a return profit to both the NRL and RFL as well as the greater game in the years ahead, with financial profits, publicity and media attention. We saw with the 2000 World Cup in England what can happen when an event runs at a major loss and how it can affect future events, investment and buy-in from all stakeholders for many years ahead.

One of the major reasons that cricket, soccer and rugby union continue to expand their international game is because it's a money driver that creates large profits, and helps build a sound financial base for each respective code and brings in plenty of media attention and interest for each sport.

Rugby league has unfortunately not had a cash cow like State of Origin or a British and Irish Lions tour off which to really expand and promote the international game, and has struggled to make a large profit on any series or tournament. Some World Cups have probably been the only events that have made some decent profits since the disastrous 2000 event, but some World Cups have also lost plenty of money and been in the red, including the last World Cup in 2021/2022.

The 2013 RLWC event was one of the more successful modern rugby league World Cups, with a profit made of approximately £3.7m, but this is nothing compared to the World Cup's massive profits for rugby union, cricket and soccer. Nonetheless, the code has plenty of untapped potential and room to grow the game and increase the financial pie and make further investment with the Ashes and more international rugby league competitions.

A revival of the Ashes series requires two great teams with fanbases which hate or dislike each other (though with great respect) to ensure its financial viability.

The game has this now, with two strong teams and plenty of new hope for the English team in 2025, and the upcoming series will see lots of strong interest in both Australia and the UK. The fans from England in particular will be baying for the Aussies' blood, which all bodes well for a tour that will capture plenty of interest and attention, especially if England perform well in the first two tests of the series.

The 2025 Ashes tour is likely to be in a much shorter format. An announcement of the 2025 Kangaroos tour has so far confirmed only the three test matches for the series across October and November, with no games announced outside of the tests, and other games unlikely to be announced before the Kangaroos depart Australia, according to British media.

The Ashes can once again become the pinnacle of the game and has the potential to become Origin-like for revenue capabilities, which would be the scorn of many in the game, but when you're leveraging both the southern hemisphere and the northern hemisphere fanbase, you're fishing in a much bigger pool, with more eyes, more television viewers, more media, bigger international companies and greater interest as a whole.

Financial Sustainability

It's not some pipe dream: you're actually dealing with mathematics, and the Ashes has the potential to match or surpass Origin and reach levels many could not imagine possible, as seen with the India/Australia cricket series in 2024-2025, the 2025 British and Irish Lions rugby tour to Australia, and the Ashes cricket in England in 2023 and 2025-26 in Australia.

A successful Ashes tour will take plenty of work and preparation both on and off the field to ensure its success, and it is critical that both the RFL/Super League and NRL are in complete alignment to maximise this coming tour and future tours to ensure their success and for them to build the foundations to become a financial powerhouse that makes a healthy profit and become established as a major event for rugby league that is locked on the calendar many years in advance.

270,000 fans attended the 18-game tour of 1994, so the foundations and potential were there back then, and those foundations still exist today, even with potentially fewer games for any future tour beyond 2025, for this to become a major event once again for the code. It is a tour that has great anticipation and excitement, that honours the history and tradition of the game and brings much prestige to the game.

I think the RFL has made a huge mistake in reverting to "England" instead of "Great Britain" for the 2025 Ashes series, despite no players likely for the team from outside of England. The name "Great Britain" is synonymous with the Ashes and British rugby league, and has a deep-rooted emotional connection with many of its own fans, who have so many great memories of the numerous famous Great Britain jumper styles over the decades, the many great players to have worn the jumper and the many great victories in that famous jersey and under that grand name who represent the best of British rugby league. All their history and tradition is under that name, and the Great Britain Lions name, like its rugby union counterpart, has real value, tradition, history and prestige in the British and international sporting landscape. The Great Britain Lions name also has real brand value that many currently involved with the game somehow don't recognise or understand, and the decision to revert to "England" for Sport England funding under former RFL Chairman Richard Lewis does not make any sense commercially, despite government funding. It is also breaking with tradition, when this will be the first Ashes series in 22 years and the first Ashes series in many, many years that will not be Great Britain against Australia. No amount of government money will ever replace or be worth all the history, prestige and tradition under the famous Great Britain Lions name, and leaders of the British game should use some common sense and revert back immediately to keep with tradition and the game's foundations.

Whilst the NRL has strong media deals with both the NRL competition and State of Origin, the missing piece of the puzzle is the international game, which has plenty of room for growth and a far larger financial return, as is seen in many other international sports.

Commercially, there is plenty of room to grow the game's international financial pie. Let's look at some of the revenue streams associated with the Ashes and more international rugby league that could provide more income in the years ahead for both the RFL/Super League and the NRL:

- Television rights
- Sponsorship
- Licensing agreements
- Government funding (major tours are winners for tourism)
- Naming rights sponsors
- Gate takings from games
- International television rights for multiple countries
- Merchandise
- Documentaries - behind the scenes
- Speaking tours
- Events and dinners

To ensure any future proper Ashes tours are successful, they must be financially profitable and sustainable for both the NRL and Super League/RFL and have room for much more growth moving forward that ensures future investment in the Ashes and more international rugby league.

The running costs associated with any future tours and expanding international rugby league schedule have also been one of the biggest anchors to the growth, expansion and real investment in the Ashes and more high-quality international rugby league, when the code currently has limited funds set aside to really invest in the sport or to fund and promote major tours, series and events.

Any short or long-term Ashes tour will come with a large operating cost, alongside the many internal and external critics. Costs can include the expenditure list below associated with any tour, and this is becoming even greater in the current inflationary cost of living crisis that is hurting so many around the world and one rugby league is not exempt from:

- Player payments
- Player allowances
- Insurances
- Flights
- Stadium fees
- Motels
- Meals
- Transportation
- Marketing and promotion
- Staff costs
- Journalists' fees
- Clothing

There are a lot of costs for any major tour between the UK and Australia, and that is why it is imperative that the NRL and Super League/RFL work in complete unity to design and create tours that will be a financial success, ensure the numbers will provide a healthy return profit, and not place the game under future threat, like was seen from the 2000 Rugby League World Cup disaster, if any debt is incurred, which is always possible with any event. There is always risk with any promotion or event, and this risk is increasing in the cost of living crisis we see today.

Far too often, the international game has not ensured tours and series maximise profit, and often this has come down to poor preparation, poor promotion and scheduling, not enough due diligence and just bad management and leadership.

Success leaves clues, and there is no mystery as to why both the British and Irish Lions rugby tours to the southern hemisphere, and the Ashes cricket series between Australia and England are so successful both on and off the field, especially financially. They know their tours will be a success many months and often years in advance, because the numbers don't lie and the groundwork and deals with key stakeholders have already been put in place, even before a ball has been bowled or a tackle made. That is what preparation and investment really are, as well as ensuring the numbers are all good and all boxes are ticked to ensure any tour's financial success and not having the fingers-crossed attitude.

The key numbers have all been ticked to ensure the tour's success, profit and future investment that helps grow the greater game many months and often years before the tour commences.

These series have major television deals in place that provide big revenue, with multiple international media providers, high attendance figures across many or all tour games that are locked in often many months and years before actual games are played, major sponsorship and government funding deals, plus other outlets that put the cherry on the cake.

Both sports know their tours will be a commercial success before any tour or series starts, as the key boxes are already ticked, and that is the position rugby league needs to get to with the Ashes and international rugby league. Sadly, it has a lot of catching up to do, after abandoning the Ashes tradition since 2003.

Multi-party media deals, large attendance numbers at games, major sponsorship, merchandise, and government funding are the foundation that pours money into both codes, and one rugby league must copy and build on with the 2025 Ashes and future series to ensure the game has a solid foundation that can grow and prosper for many years to come.

That's all rugby league has to do to ensure the Ashes once again becomes the pinnacle of the sport and is commercially viable and can help support the reduction of Super League and NRL club games, as the revenue capabilities for an Ashes series and tour far outweigh club game capabilities, as seen with the 2025 British and Irish Lions tour Down Under. It really is maximum leverage when you have a far wider fan base and in much bigger numbers and interest compared to any regular season club game, and one that major sports such as cricket, soccer and rugby union with international audiences know all about and use to their advantage.

Future Ashes series, starting with the upcoming 2025 series, will be beginning at the bottom of the mountain once again, and will have to probably be run very lean to ensure a profit and success, but I have no doubt that over time and with the right investment and leadership, future tours can match and possibly exceed what cricket and rugby union have done in recent years. But the key commercial arrangements must be the foundation for its longevity and success, and this must be locked in many years in advance. The code should be looking at locking in future series immediately after the 2025 series and commencing planning for all facets of future Ashes tours, which will allow for maximum time to promote and invest in future Ashes series and build key strategic partnerships.

The supply/demand element for the Ashes makes it so attractive when you are only playing three tests every 2 years and possibly only visiting England or Australia once every 4 years. That scarcity value, compared to 27 Super League or NRL games per year, makes it special and unique, and of a much higher value to the code.

That's why it is critical to have all parties working in complete unity, from selecting the right stadiums to promoting test matches well to ensure that games are sold out, selecting the right tour games against club teams that will gain plenty of coverage and attention, and attract large crowds to give tours some publicity buzz and ensure maximum profit, locking in media deals outside the current arrangements to provide new sources of revenue that can ensure the future of the Ashes and more international rugby league. Working with government to promote international and domestic tourism and major sponsorship to grow each national brand is a win-win partnership to managing all costs associated with any tour, to ensure tours run at a profit and not over budget.

Strong finances must be the bedrock for the 2025 Ashes series and any future series. We know rugby league is an exciting game to watch; now we must lock in media deals for series and tours, fill big stadiums and club games and regrow the brands of both England/Great Britain and Australia to attract the biggest sponsorships available, as well as partner with government to boost local economies and support touring fans and manage all expenses associated with any tour to ensure that any Ashes tour does not run at a loss. Rugby union and cricket have both done this, and now rugby league must follow their lead and start building the foundations once again for the Ashes revival and more international rugby league.

CUSTODIANS FOR THE INTERNATIONAL GAME

WHILE THIS BOOK is predominantly about supporting and advocating for the revival of the Ashes series and the longer format tours associated with any Ashes series, I also strongly believe that both Australia and England must play the lead role in being custodians for the greater game and helping it grow in other countries around the world, which is a huge responsibility but one that they are both qualified for and must do for the wellbeing and future of the sport.

They say a rising tide lifts all boats, and only Australia and England have the resources, finances, media deals and capabilities to raise the sport around the world.

The game of rugby league really has only two elite professional leagues in the world, being the NRL and Super League, which are based in Australia and England, with teams from New Zealand and France in respective competitions.

The game can't really grow internationally without financial resources, and only big countries such as Australia and England, with their ability to attract major media deals, can drive more income at this time into the code, which can then be reinvested back into the sport.

There is no doubt that some great stuff has happened in recent years around the world, from France with the Catalans Dragons and Toulouse doing their best to revive the French game, and now Carcassonne is following a similar path, with a burning desire to follow in their footsteps and join the English Championship League. Wales has seen a lot of good work at the domestic level after years of lost opportunity since the 1995 World Cup, when it had the world at its feet but lost its way. It is now building a good foundation that should be the model for other nations and will hopefully reap good fruit in the years ahead. New Zealand has seen a wave of new support in recent years with Warrior games selling out fast and becoming the hottest ticket in town and becoming even more popular than the mighty All Blacks, with the Wahs' slogan becoming the biggest thing in NZ sport and entertainment, to the Pacific nations, which have seen a wave of support since Tonga's 2017 strong World Cup performance and Samoa's 2022 World Cup, where they reached the final against Australia with a wave of local support both home and abroad, and now PNG, who continue to improve at all levels of the game and who have now been confirmed entry into the NRL competition in 2028.

Behind the scenes, many volunteers are working hard to set up leagues in places many would not be aware the game is played: Greece, Lebanon, Kenya, Brazil, Norway, Ireland, Scotland, and Serbia each doing their bit to grow and improve the code and laying the seeds for future generations to come that will hopefully lead to rugby league becoming a recognised and popular sport in each country.

Many would argue that on the back of the incredible success from Pacific nations since 2017, they can lead the way for the code, but whilst they have done a terrific job and increased the profile and appetite for more international rugby league, one must not forget that most of the players selected for such countries as Tonga and Samoa are not born in these countries and they are utilising the grandparent rule for eligibility, when nearly all players are still Australian or NZ born and raised.

Tonga and Samoa do not have the financial resources to spread the rugby league gospel or drive major international media deals. Tonga has a population of only 105,000 and Samoa's population is around 220,000, with both teams still playing international games either in New Zealand or Australia, as games are only attractive and financially viable in New Zealand or Australia at this stage without financial subsidies from governments or the NRL or NZRL.

Fiji and Papua New Guinea are more advanced, with both teams now hosting international games in Port Moresby and Suva. But they both still lack the resources and financial capabilities to really grow and support the game around the world.

Only Australia and England really have the capabilities and resources to drive the game, and they should both lead the game's growth in both the northern hemisphere and the southern hemisphere.

The two keys functions to being custodians and leaders for the game of rugby league around the world, I think, are rebuilding their own national brands on the international scene and making the Ashes the greatest rivalry in rugby league once again, which will then flow on for the desire for more international rugby league between other nations and create a dynamic international scene.

Secondly, as stated before, it is supporting neighbouring nations to grow the sport, with Australia leading the way in the southern hemisphere with such countries as New Zealand, PNG, Fiji, Tonga, Samoa, and the Cook Islands, which all have plenty of room for more growth and development. I am not a fan of the grandparent rule, despite the many supporters, and believe it devalues both State of Origin and representation in the international game. I believe the better long-term investment is in developing better domestic leagues for both men and women, the school system, pathway programmes, and resources for staff to coach, and professional management to manage and administer the sport and other investment strategies to grow the sport around the world.

Papua New Guinea's current model in the southern hemisphere, which is only behind Australia and New Zealand, is one that countries such as Tonga, Samoa, the Cook Islands and Fiji should be aiming for.

What about the opportunities with Argentina and South Africa? Both of these nations are now powerhouse teams in world rugby union, and rugby league still has no real presence in either country, despite rugby's enormous popularity in both countries, especially South Africa.

South Africa has won the last two Rugby World Cups, with many considering their current team one of the best of all time. The country is loaded with talent, with the South African school system now regarded as one of the best nurseries for rugby talent in the world, one where so many young players would be suited for rugby league, and yet many are not even aware of the code. There are no born and bred South African rugby league players in Super League or the NRL and very little domestic rugby league infrastructure in South Africa today.

Argentina, once known and still known as a soccer giant, is another potential future growth spot for the code. With famous players such as Diego Maradona and Lionel Messi playing for Argentina, rugby has now surged in popularity, with the national team reaching the semi-finals of the 2023 World Cup in France, and in recent years winning test matches at home and abroad against Australia, New Zealand and South Africa.

Argentina's and Japan's rise up the world rugby ladder should be a reminder to rugby league leaders of what is possible with belief, long-term planning, determination and persistence.

In the northern hemisphere, which is overshadowed by soccer and rugby union's dominance, England should take the lead to promote and grow the sport in the region, or at least until the code has the money, resources and sound administration with the IRL to take charge of the game globally to distribute money and resources that align with a strategic plan for international rugby league.

The Ashes - *Rugby League's Most Important Rivalry*

Obvious opportunities for England include their UK neighbors such as Ireland, Scotland and Wales. This would be great for England to see these nations start producing more high-quality players, as this would improve and strengthen Great Britain and grow the game more across the United Kingdom.

A stronger UK and Ireland has many benefits for the English team, including a stronger Great Britain team, more people following and watching the sport, which could lead to bigger media deals, and a bigger profile like the one rugby union has today in the UK.

One thing I am happy to see with all three in Scotland, Ireland and Wales is the move away from the silly grandparent rule selections for World Cups, which is a top-down approach, with a focus now on getting more UK born and raised boys and girls to play the sport, improving domestic leagues and developing pathways for talented players to scale higher up the system. Already we have seen a number of Irish and Welsh born and raised players make their way to Super League, and hopefully we will see many more in the years ahead, with the national teams being made up of UK players in future World Cups, not those born and raised in Australia who qualify through the grandparent rule, despite never living or working in these countries.

France is obviously a country that needs major support, a country with so much potential and history with the game, which has faced enormous adversity during the Vichy era and yet can never reach its potential due to internal stakeholder and management issues that continue to plague the game and its growth.

Other nations in the north which look to have great potential include Serbia, Greece and Lebanon, which all look to be building some solid domestic leagues that are growing in popularity, and, who knows, may become rugby league countries like Japan or Argentina have become for rugby union in the years ahead and would be a breath of fresh air for the sport if the code could develop a deeper international playing pool.

The Ashes is where it all starts, the greatest rivalry in international rugby league, the history and tradition of the game and the future for the game.

Both England and Australia should honour tradition and the jersey by making the Ashes a priority once again. From the revival and rebirth of the Ashes in 2025, it is only natural that the game will see the overwhelming benefits and more demand, and want to take responsibility to further grow the game around the world.

KEY PARTIES - FRANCE/WALES/ NEW ZEALAND/ PACIFIC NATIONS

IN THE LAST chapter, we talked about how Australia and England must become custodians for the game and take the lead in promoting and growing the sport around the world.

While this book is predominantly about the restoration and revival of the grandest rivalry in rugby league, the Ashes between Australia and England/Great Britain, there are some key stakeholders outside of this grand rivalry who hold significant short-term and long-term importance for both nations in each respective hemisphere and for the health of the Ashes and international rugby league as a whole.

For England, it is imperative that both France and Wales continue to grow and become much stronger, both on and off the field, as England has limited options to play quality international teams in the northern hemisphere in the present climate, which would help the sport in the UK and Europe significantly and provide quality competition outside of the Ashes, with preparation for other international series and to create competition between each other that could grow into something of significance and interest to fans from each nation.

A strong French and Welsh national team also enhances future Ashes tours. During the 1994 Ashes tour, Australia played test matches against both Wales and France. It is imperative that these nations improve quickly so future tour matches can be scheduled, which will make the Ashes and the tour itself even bigger in profile and excitement.

Currently, England, sadly, only has France as possible opponents in the northern hemisphere who can provide some decent competition, but in recent years, these games have been one-sided affairs, with France's last victory over Great Britain coming way back in 1990 in the second test match at Headingley with a 25-18 victory. The last two decades have seen England completely dominate the French, with little improvement seen from the French, despite the inclusion of the Catalans Dragons in Super League and the emergence of Toulouse as a professional club in France.

Such has been the disappointment with mid-year and end-of-season test matches against the French, that many within the British game are now calling for the return of the War of Roses game between Yorkshire and Lancashire to help prepare the national team for higher quality opponents. I strongly disagree with this and firmly believe much more work must be done to help the French game, and that it is of vital importance that investment and commitment is shown to both the French and Welsh, with annual fixtures against England.

Rugby league needs a strong French team, but despite the clear potential, the results have been disappointment after disappointment, from the cancellation of the 2025 World Cup, when the French would have hosted the cup, which would have been a wonderful boost for French rugby league and for the game to finally break the British and Australian/NZ/PNG stranglehold for hosting the event, but later had to be cancelled due to funding issues with the French Government, the international team's poor performance over many years with little signs of improvement, its terrible record against England, and the lack of growth and profile for the sport in a country where soccer and rugby union continue to dominate. The game still only has pockets of interest in the south of the country and is still operating very amateurishly, compared with other professional sports.

Many still talk about the Vichy government banning rugby league and seizing all its assets during World War Two, which was terrible for the code, but 80 years have now lapsed since that dreadful period, and the blame lies with French authorities, who have been unable to grow and promote the sport. It is still only played in pockets in the south of France, with little or no real growth seen and no major media deals to really enhance the game and make it a major sport.

The French game has seen a wave of different committees and leaders come and go in the last 50 years, all unable to revitalise the code or catch a glimpse of glory from the majestic 1950s period when the French at their pinnacle were able to defeat Australia twice on tours on Australian soil, with such famous players as Puig Albert and Ellie Brousse.

England or Great Britain badly need a strong French team to provide some real competition that can help regrow the international game, provide England with some quality competition in the north and create its own rivalry between both nations, as seen in rugby union.

In 2024, the French u19s team completed a tour of Australia, which included games against Australian club teams and the Australian Schoolboys, though they were hammered 56-6 by the Australian Schoolboys. This is a wonderful experience and a reality check on what it takes to make it as a professional rugby league player, and can only benefit French rugby league in the years ahead.

Despite the one-sided scorelines in that test and some other matches, these tours are the exact exposure and experience the young French players need if they are to become seasoned professional players who can compete at the elite level and change the culture and professionalism of the French game.

Sydney Roosters coach Trent Robinson, a former Catalans Dragons coach who married a French woman, was one of the driving forces behind the tour, and is intent on helping rebuild the French game and build the game from the bottom up with pathway programmes.

Whilst the French game struggles for a bigger profile and a bigger media presence, some of the most promising news was the French U19s win over the England Academy in 2024, with a thrilling 40-37 win at Warrington, which included a number of England players who had played Super League in 2024 with more debutants from the team in 2025. This is probably the first time in a long time when the French are starting to have talent that could push up the professional ranks and play Super League or NRL, which is healthy for the French and for world rugby league.

Whether England likes it or not, they are partners with the French and not off-field competitors, as many think within the English game. The Catalans Dragons are now one of Super League's stronger clubs, and Toulouse is fighting hard to win back a place in Super League. With Toulouse being a major city, it has plenty of admirers from IMG, with its potential as a long-term Super League franchise. And now Carcassonne, who have dominated the local French game, have announced they plan to enter the Rugby League Championship in the years ahead.

Rugby league needs a strong French team, and England benefits from this more than any other country. We need a strong local French competition that is expanding and growing around the country and moving beyond its southern roots into the bigger cities. We need media deals that provide revenue and much greater exposure for the game to grow its profile and fan base, we need new French talent that become household names, and England should partner with the French to support and invest in any way they can.

At the 1995 Rugby League World Cup, Wales looked to be on the rise, with the team reaching the semi-finals of the event with a host of code converts in the team, only to lose to arch rivals England at Old Trafford in Manchester 25-10 in front of over 30,000 fans in a highly competitive match.

Wales saw excellent home crowds at both Cardiff and Swansea during the 1995 tournament and were boosted by the signing of several Welsh international rugby players, which created plenty of publicity and exposure, as they performed strongly across the tournament to reach the semi-finals. A new dawn for Welsh rugby league looked incredibly promising at that point in time.

Those great hopes of a Welsh renaissance quickly turned to disappointment when rugby union turned professional around 1995. The game has never quite reached those lofty heights again, as rugby union surged past its rugby league counterpart to retain prominence in Wales and the UK.

For whatever reasons, the code has been unable to build a really strong foundation over the last 30 years in the rugby mad nation, with rugby union remaining the nation's strongest sport. It is religion-like in many ways for the public, though some pundits would say there are a number of cracks growing in the Welsh game, as seen with the current game in New Zealand.

Some would argue that Wales, Ireland and New Zealand all have similarities for their passion and pride in their national rugby union teams.

The 2000 Rugby League World Cup saw the Welsh team again make the semi-finals of the cup when they performed strongly, and nearly provided one of the biggest upsets in rugby league history when they took a big lead against the

Kangaroos, before eventually being run down, to lose 46 to 22. The team benefitted from the grandparent rule. With most players English-born, they did not capture the Welsh public's interest like the 1995 World Cup, despite the strong on-field results.

The team did not qualify for the 2008 World Cup in Australia, and finished last in its pool in the 2013 World Cup, hosted again in the UK, losing all three games. They again lost all three group games 4 years later at the 2017 World Cup in Australia.

The team would perform admirably, despite again losing all three games in the 2021/22 World Cup held in England, placed in a very tough pool with Tonga, PNG and the Cook Islands, but won plenty of admirers and respect from the Welsh public for their gritty performances in the three defeats.

Many thought the entry of a professional Welsh team in Super League based in Wales would reverse the code's fortunes and provide the kickstart needed for Welsh rugby league, with the Celtic Crusaders joining Super League in 2009, based at Bridgend, and then later at Wrexham. But the team sadly collapsed after just 3 years at the end of 2011. Over the 3 years, the club averaged 3,820 attendees per game, with a season high of 4,416 for the 2010 season. Financial difficulties were the reason for the club's collapse in September 2011, when the club owner pulled the pin.

The club would later be reformed under the name of the North Wales Crusaders, who are now based at Colwyn Bay and playing in League One, and have had some good results in recent years in front of decent crowds, as they look to make their way to the Rugby League Championship across the UK rugby league landscape.

There were many reasons for the failure of the Celtic Crusaders, which also sums up the health of Welsh rugby league at the time, including the financial difficulties of the owners, who would end up winding the team up, the lack of local born and bred Welsh players, with many of the players coming from Australia to make up the squad during those 3 years, the team not capturing the hearts and minds of the Welsh public, the team not being based in Cardiff, which is the country's capital and economic power base where the major companies and investors are all based and with a much larger population compared with the more regional towns of Bridgend and Wrexham, and poor junior numbers and weak domestic leagues at the time.

In many ways, the game in Wales had no sound foundation, and a top-down approach with a bunch of Aussie expats was never going to find lasting success or win the hearts and minds of the Welsh public in this rugby mad nation.

As hard as the downfall and failures of the Celtic Crusaders and the poor on-field results for the national team have been since the 2000 World Cup, I think there are plenty of reasons to be optimistic about the future of Welsh rugby league in the years ahead

Despite losing all three games at the 2021/22 World Cup, there was plenty of spirit shown, and I think the code in Wales is now headed in the right direction, with a view to the long-term rather than short-term success. Twelve of the 24 players from the last World Cup were born and raised in Wales, and this is a promising start in the revival of the game, when local born and raised players are pulling on the national jumper.

After the 1995 tournament high, which was boosted with the big name union code converts, the code has never reached those lofty heights again or gone close to winning the hearts and minds of the nation, despite some brief moments of joy in World Cup games.

Wales has now gone back to the basics and decided to rebuild the game from the ground up and build a strong foundation at the base. I think they will see success in the long term with such a strategy, if they remain persistent and committed to growing the game.

Picking players on the grandparent rule, many of whom have never spent any time in Wales, is not going to grow the game. It may provide brief moments of success during a World Cup, but it will never appeal to the Welsh public or attract major media attention to provide the code with a larger profile. I think leaders within the Welsh game have now recognised this and have adequately changed course in recent years.

The Welsh game's foundations are now been rebuilt, with a focus on attracting more Welsh youth to play the game, with a particular priority on junior growth and participation across the boys', women's and disability games, and there are already some promising signs, with player numbers reaching over 4,000 in 2024, a 4.5% increase on 2023, 46% on 2022 and a huge 201% from 2021, reported Welsh rugby league in late 2024.

Pathway programmes have also been set up, with Wales

Juniors in both the boys', women's and disability sectors now playing regularly against international competition. A professional career in rugby league is more than a possibility for any young talented players who are willing to do the hard work and chase their dream.

I said in my book *Crossroads - Rugby League's Greatest Battle (2023)* that rugby league had huge potential for growth in rugby mad New Zealand, and that prediction has proven true, as the code has seen a second wave of surging popularity from 2024, with many now believing the code could become the number one rugby code in New Zealand, which was inconceivable to many casual sporting fans not so long ago. I also sense that if rugby league can get its own house in order in Wales, there are also huge opportunities for growth in this rugby union mad nation, and rugby league can finally get a foothold. The game of rugby union is off the nose with the Welsh public after years of disappointing on-field performance and off-field disputes. There seems to be a gulf between fans and the Welsh Rugby Union and its players, and rugby league in Wales now has another chance to seize the moment, if they do things right and lay the right foundations. Plenty of work needs to be done over the next decade if this is to occur, but make no mistake, there is a huge opportunity for Welsh rugby league to re-emerge as a national sport in Wales.

This bottom-up approach is a long-term strategy which will take many years to bear fruit, but it is the only model that can have sustainable long-term success that can also win the hearts and minds of the Welsh public and push Wales back up the rankings for the international game and grow the profile for the sport.

Already some seeds are starting to bear fruit, with a number of local Welsh born and bred juniors being signed up by Super League clubs, and Salford now has a strategic partnership with the Welsh to provide a pathway for talented juniors, as part of an agreement with the Wales Development Academy.

Wales, unfortunately, did not qualify for the 2026 World Cup in Australia, losing to France 48-6 in Carcassonne in late 2024. I think this is very harsh, and former coach of the national team, John Kear's criticism of cup organisers is full of merit, with the competition reduced from 16 teams to 10 teams for the 2026 World Cup.

While we see many nations exploit the grandparent rule to select and strengthen national teams, with Tonga, Samoa, the Cook Islands, and Lebanon squads nearly all made up of players born and raised outside of these countries, they are represented with most of the squad coming from either Australia and New Zealand, with many players also having played State of Origin, or, in some cases, with another country and then swapping allegiances, which is making a mockery of the rules, and one officials need to sort out asap, as it becomes more and more confusing and jeopardises the integrity of the sport.

Rather than reward countries for the development and growth of more players that are born and raised locally, and stronger domestic leagues, which is the path Wales is going down, the current system and international governing body rewards only on-field performance, which is sponsored and supported with the grandparent rule, as seen with Lebanon,

Tonga, Samoa, the Cook Islands and many other countries, despite many of these nations having little in the way of domestic leagues or a strong local playing base.

We have seen the emergence of Argentina, Japan, Georgia and Portugal in rugby union, and they are not built on the grandparent rule but rather, from a bottom-up approach that develops local players, building stronger domestic leagues and pathway systems for talented players, and then the utilises the national team to grow the brand and profile of the sport to a much bigger global audience.

This is the exact approach and long-term view that Wales is now taking, and I strongly believe Wales and other countries which focus on juniors and domestic leagues should be rewarded and supported for growing the sport, rather than the lazy grandparent rule eligibility that does little to grow the game with more juniors and stronger domestic leagues, but only improves on-field performances and provides fleeting moments of success.

Some would counter-argue to look at Tonga's and Samoa's impact on the international game, and I would agree they have played a key part in the revival and desire for more international rugby league. But this is worthless if they have no local juniors or domestic leagues and no ability to play games in their home nations. Japan's and Argentina's recent success are the models rugby league officials must be following to ensure the growth of the international game and long-term success for rugby league

We need a strong Welsh national team, and we again need a Welsh team back in Super League, once the foundations are stronger with more local players and stronger domestic leagues and more interest in the game as a whole from the Welsh public. We need big rugby league games and internationals played at Millenium Stadium Cardiff and in other cities across the country.

England badly needs other northern hemisphere opponents who can provide stiff competition outside of the powerhouse southern hemisphere nations, which can help promote and grow the international game. Wales, like France, is the perfect partner.

I still remember the excitement and build-up to the 1995 semi-final between England and Wales at Old Trafford, and believe those days can once again come, and a new dawn with this rivalry can emerge, with the investment in youth and domestic leagues from both Wales and the French.

Both France and Wales have a long history with rugby league, with France hosting the first World Cup in 1954, and Wales being one of the earliest countries to play rugby league, and which has a fascinating history with the sport, and a great rivalry with England.

Wales and France are critical partners for England to strengthen the northern hemisphere game, expand and boost future Ashes tours, strengthen Great Britain and add much more depth and interest to the international game. It is imperative that France and Wales improve, for the sake of Australia and England, the Ashes tours and the international game, and all support and resources must be provided and invested to make this a reality.

Whilst New Zealand may be the third strongest nation

Key Parties - France/Wales/New Zealand/Pacific Nations

for world rugby league, they are still a crucial partner for Australia, Pacific nations and even their northern hemisphere counterparts for supporting the growth of international rugby league.

The NZ Warriors are currently riding a wave of momentum across the country that has not been seen since the club's entry into the ARL competition in 1995, but this wave of support has not yet fully transferred to the national team's popularity, who, in their own right, have an incredible history with the code, with many great moments that have helped shaped the code in the country.

Rugby union, which is like a religion in NZ, is facing some of its toughest times in many years, after an era of unparalleled success, which included winning the 2011 and 2015 World Cups.

The All Blacks are still the number one ticket in town, but that aura of invincibility they once had both on and off the field is losing its shine in these changing times.

The code is off the nose with many fans, and the Warriors are currently making huge gains in the once dominated rugby union stronghold across the country. Many fans think the code has lost its heart and soul after signing part of its ownership to an American investment firm, Silver Lake, in 2022 for NZ$200 million. To many fans, the famous black jersey has lost its soul and is now all about money and global brand recognition, that it is only concerned with profits and has lost touch with many of the working class fans across New Zealand.

New Zealand Rugby lost $19.5 million in 2024, despite

record earnings, and is NZR's third consecutive deficit, following a $8.9m loss in 2023 and a $47m loss in 2022.

Super Rugby across Australasia is in a rut, with the game unsure how to move forward with both South African and Australian clubs, and is in a transitional phase for the code, with many worried about the future for the competition, despite Australian clubs' improvement in recent years. Many of New Zealand's best players in recent years have signed contracts with clubs from all around the world, including France, Ireland, England and Japan, which has further diluted the domestic competition, the traditional pathway to the All Blacks.

New Zealand Rugby League must take full advantage of rugby union's struggles. The national team is a critical component to make further gains in the NZ sporting market and support the Warriors' surging popularity. The Kiwis, as many call the national team, has probably taken a backseat to Tonga and Samoa in recent years and has been hurt by players swapping allegiances, poor on-field performances despite winning the 2023 Pacific Cup against Australia, inactivity, and, like England and Australia with the Ashes, lack of meaningful series played in prime time at home and abroad that captures the public's attention.

Despite New Zealand winning the World Cup in 2008 against Australia 34-20 and winning a number of international series and the 2023 Pacific Cup tournament since then, the rivalry between Australia and New Zealand has never reached its full potential or come close to matching the popularity of the Bledisloe Cup in rugby union between the same countries.

I think there are a number of reasons why this has occurred, and they have been touched upon in this book: Inactivity, poor scheduling, poor leadership, no meaningful head-to-head series are just a few key reasons for its unfulfilled potential. As stated, to revive the rivalry between the Kiwis and Australia like the Ashes, it needs quality competition, which both teams have in abundance, played in meaningful series and tournaments, and a scheduled itinerary many years in advance, with strong marketing, and the results will come both on and off the field.

Australia needs to grow the rivalry once again with its brothers from New Zealand.

The best way for the Kiwis to regrow their own national team's brand and popularity across New Zealand is to play the Kangaroos every year in three-game series, or, at a minimum, once every 2 years, which could also be mixed in alternatively with tournaments involving Pacific nations teams, as we have seen in the last 2 years with the Pacific Cup. However, I strongly believe a regular head-to-head series against Australia is a must for the sport and both countries to grow the game and this great rivalry.

Like the Ashes, the trans-Tasman rivalry between the Kangaroos and Kiwis is so undervalued, despite so much shared history between both countries. It has so much more potential, especially with the high number of Kiwi players in the NRL today and the sport's rising popularity in NZ. There is no reason to believe that this clash could not match and exceed the Bledisloe Cup in terms of popularity, if played in a meaningful series and scheduled regularly each year. It has all the makings of another wow event!

The three-game Tasman series against Australia is the perfect fit to support the Ashes in reviving meaningful international head-to-head series, and provides both countries with topline competition that will improve growing their national brands and the international game as a whole and help further reduce the dependence on NRL club games for television revenue. It will grow the international game's financial pie with more events that capture the fans' attention.

New Zealand is a critical partner for Australia to provide meaningful head-to-head series with each year and grow this rivalry, which can take the sport in New Zealand to a whole new level. They give England and Great Britain competition when not playing Australia, and they also have the ability to expand and build competition and rivalry with the other Pacific nations such as Tonga, Samoa, Fiji and Papua New Guinea, in either tri or quad format competitions or head-to-head series, which makes them an incredibly important stakeholder in the future of international rugby league.

The Pacific nations of Papua New Guinea, Samoa, Tonga, Fiji and the Cook Islands are also important partners for Australia and the growth of the international game. Over the last decade, we have seen significant improvement from all Pacific nations, which has played a key role in the revival and interest for more international rugby league. The Pacific Cup and Pacific Bowl competitions at the end of the NRL season in 2023 and 2024 have been well received, and Samoa and

Tonga have both toured England over the last 2 years to solidify Pacific nations as international playing countries.

Continual improvement must be the mantra moving forward and to keep building on the good foundations that have been laid in recent years. Papua New Guinea is the most developed of the Pacific nations. This rugby league mad nation has seen the establishment of a Queensland Cup team, a soon-to-be NRL team from 2028, developed infrastructure, which includes a major stadium in Port Moresby, strong government support, plus strong domestic leagues and pathway programmes with plenty of emerging talent, with the PNG Junior Kumuls pushing the Junior Kangaroos to a draw in 2024. This all bodes well for the future of the sport in the country.

After winning the Pacific Bowl in 2024, PNG should now be aiming to step up and play regular high-level competition at home and abroad against the game's best in Australia, New Zealand and England. If Papua New Guinea can keep improving and developing more of the local talent, tours to the UK to play England, Wales and France, and series against Australia and New Zealand could all become commercially attractive for the game.

For the remaining Pacific nations, it's all about building the foundations that will last for many years to come, with much work still to be done, despite some incredible on-field success from Tonga, Fiji and Samoa in the last two World Cups and the huge following the Pacific nations have attracted, where fans are now outnumbering Australian and New Zealand fans at home games. Outside of PNG, and Fiji to a lesser degree, other Pacific nations are still heavily dependent on the grandparent rule for on-field success, and this top-down approach is not a sustainable model for the code if those rules are removed in the years ahead. These Pacific nations need to be focused on building the foundations across the game from stronger domestic leagues, school and youth programmes, pathways for talented youth, infrastructure and facilities development to be able to host international games, and sound administration to manage the game and become fiscally and commercially attractive with a sound financial base.

In the movie *Field of Dreams*, they say, "If you build it, they will come." If the code keeps building on what they have across the Pacific, the fruits will be well worth it in the years ahead. Australia should continue to play the lead role in the Pacific game's growth and development.

A strong Pacific group of rugby league playing nations increases the depth of international rugby league and the quality of the Pacific Cup and Pacific Bowl, adds the option for future head-to-head series between nations, and provides England/Great Britain with more touring options Down Under and the option for Pacific nations to tour the UK, as seen in 2023 and 2024 with Tonga and Samoa.

Wales, France, New Zealand and the other Pacific nations are all critical parts of the overall health and future success of international rugby league. If they keep growing and developing, this boosts Ashes tours, increases international depth and options for head-to-head and other series, and makes the World Cup so much more attractive to the fans.

EXISTENTIAL CRISIS

HISTORIANS SAY THAT when a nation or empire forgets its roots, history, culture and traditions, it quickly declines and collapses from within, with history books littered with examples of once strong empires and countries which have collapsed over the last 6,000 years of recorded history.

Rugby league in both Australia and England has had its own existential crisis in recent times, forgetting the history and tradition of the game and how the past provides a light and path for the future that keeps the game connected through the generations and changing times.

The Ashes is the antidote to any existential crisis from within the game. It honours the past, keeps traditions alive, and keeps the bond and special relationship between Australia and England, which have been inseparably linked from the game's earliest beginnings, as also seen with cricket since the first Ashes test match in 1877, which is still as strong as ever today, despite the many changes and challenges from that period.

To move forward, you always have to honour the past and understand what has made this game so special and unique. Nothing epitomises rugby league more so than the best of England or the United Kingdom in Great Britain facing off against the best from Australia in an Ashes series.

Rugby league was born in Huddersfield in 1895 when the code broke away from rugby union, with the game of rugby league commencing in Sydney, Australia in 1908.

The first Ashes series was played across 1908/1909, with the Northern Union (England/Great Britain) hosting Australia and winning the series 2-0. Since that initial series, Ashes series have been played between both countries both at home and abroad up until 2003, with 1994 being the last longer conventional tour, with some gap years during this period due to outbreak of wars during the 20th century.

Is it any surprise then, that the code has struggled to keep pace with its rugby rivals on the international scene, when in the last two to three decades, the very foundation and tradition of the sport has been forsaken and forgotten?

Many newer fans of the game today forget or are completely unaware of the Super League war in the mid-1990s that ripped the heart and soul out of the game in Australia, and to some degree also in England, and how, despite all the millions spent and the promises made with television deals and money, the game was becoming meaningless to many fans. It had lost what had made it great to many followers of the sport. It seemed it had all become about money and there was no heart and soul or connection with the fans. Even the English game has seen this, with many fans critical of governing bodies and some club owners for putting the clubs and profit before honouring the tradition and foundation of the game when the code signed with BSkyB in 1996.

It has taken many years for the game to recover from the Super League war, which was a horrendous period in the game's history. The scars remain and some wounds will never heal.

The Kangaroo tours and Ashes series in many ways were unfortunately the scapegoats for this upheaval and the healing process in the years after, which became club and league focused in both hemispheres, at the expense of Ashes series and extended tours.

Many fans walked away from the game during this period when money seemed to be all the game was about, and tradition and history were forsaken. The code had lost its bond and connection with many of the working class fan base. That must never happen again.

That period in the game is still a great warning for the code when it looks to make more money via television, gambling, government and other sources, and forgets its roots and history and relationship with the fans.

The Ashes series is the greatest rivalry in the code that honours both past and present and the two great founding nations of rugby league in both hemispheres, and it must be restored to its rightful place as the pinnacle for the sport.

Hopefully, the upcoming 2025 Ashes series will reignite

the love, passion, excitement and hatred that only an Ashes series can provide, and will lead to a whole new exciting dawn for England/Great Britain vs Australia and the Ashes series and the return of extended tours for many years to come.

EPILOGUE

AFTER WRITING AND releasing *Crossroads - Rugby League's Greatest Battle in 2023*, I promised myself that I would never write another book about rugby league and would focus on other matters of interest in my life. The reason I wrote that book was, as a lifelong fan of the game, I felt there were many risks to the future of rugby league in Australia that needed to be addressed that were not being written about and that had not been discussed or addressed in the media and were vitally important to the code's long-term future and success.

Whilst rugby league has bounced back quite well from COVID, I still believe wholeheartedly that what I wrote about in *Crossroads* and the subjects I discussed are still as relevant as ever in 2025. Although some issues that I wrote about have been addressed to some degree, there are still many that plague the game and are real threats to its long-term health and future, despite the Australian game looking strong to many from the outside.

The seeds of this book and project slowly started to sprout whilst watching many Super League games over the last few seasons. I have always had a genuine love for the British game and want to see it succeed, and I, like many fans, have been frustrated that governance battles, stakeholder infighting, poor strategy, poor execution and leadership issues have all played a part in holding the British game back from more mainstream popularity that the code badly deserves after a renaissance of the British game in the early 1990s.

I love the British game, the crowds, the famous clubs, the great stadiums that feel so close to the action, the noise and singing from the fans and the style of rugby, which is far less structured than the NRL product.

Despite the many criticisms from Australian fans and experts, in recent years, I have found the British game to be far more enjoyable than the NRL, despite many believing the NRL is far superior and of higher quality. The British game for me is better entertainment than the NRL, with it having much more unpredictability, passion and excitement, which goes totally against popular opinion.

I still don't understand why the RFL and Super League want to copy and follow everything the NRL does. They should pave their own path and have much more confidence in the British game and their own ideals. They need to remember the British did invent rugby league way back in 1895 and they created a game that still stands today and has survived across wars, depressions, political and social change and challenges from other sports and still continues to grow and spread around the world.

The NRL, to me, has become dull and boring in recent times, with repetitive second-man plays in attack, all too much structure in both attack and defence, continual bombs on the last tackle to the corner in attack, video referee interference that stops all momentum and spectacle enjoyment, and wrestling to slow and control the ruck. Also, there is the influence of gambling everywhere. This has eroded my trust and confidence in the integrity of the game, when one can now bet on anything which does not even include the end score or winner of a game. This has been exacerbated with the implementation of the six again rule, maybe the most dangerous rule change in the sport's history, which can now swing the momentum of a game like no rule the game has ever seen before, and where the referees are not held accountable for their decisions that can determine the outcome of many or all games.

Many British fans probably don't realise just how special the UK game really is. Pessimism is often all too common with many fans and stakeholders. There is all the great history and tradition and rivalries from the beginning of the sport: the great clubs of Wigan, St Helens, Leeds, Warrington, Hull, and Hull KR, to the modern day battlers like Castleford, Leigh, Huddersfield, Salford, and Wakefield, to London who continue to fight for the game in the south, to the expansion of teams from France, who have added a new layer to the sport, and the excitement of promotion and relegation, which many don't want today. I don't understand this, in many ways, when it is part of your history and culture and provides a pathway for all clubs to dream and hope of being a Super League club. When you remove this, you become a dream killer.

I think the Rugby League Championship is a great competition, with some of the most famous clubs in British rugby league and has so much more potential, and hopefully, once all clubs strengthen both on and off the field, we will see the return of promotion and relegation between both Super League and the Rugby League Championship. York, Bradford, Toulouse and London all have great untapped potential and would add great value to Super League.

After taking some time to reflect on how much I admire and love the British game and the Ashes, I felt it was only right, and my duty to advocate for a return of the Ashes, rugby league's greatest and most important rivalry, and write a book about it. It really is the most important rivalry in the entire sport!

Unlike the Ashes in cricket, which seems to get bigger and bigger with the public each series, the complete opposite has occurred with the Ashes in rugby league. I felt something needed to be said about the return of the Ashes, alongside advocating for the traditional longer format tours, which would bring so much excitement and history back to the game.

Rugby league's greatest rivalry has been dormant for far too long, and this inactivity has hurt the game significantly in both countries, as the national team profiles of other codes gain more traction and attention.

When I was a young fan, the Ashes was the pinnacle for the code, and I can still recall the wonderful period for the

Epilogue

game between 1988 and 1995 and the many great games during this time, and the optimism for international rugby league, when anything looked possible for the code, before the Super League war.

I miss the Kangaroos tours and watching the Kangaroos play club sides like Wigan, Leeds and St Helens, the tour games against Wales and France, and of course I miss getting up early to watch the big test matches at Wembley, Leeds or Old Trafford.

I miss Great Britain or England not having properly toured Australia since 1992, playing local and professional teams and the three big test matches. I miss a strong Great Britain/England team with big name star players, though I do think the potential is there now for the English to do the impossible and upset the Kangaroos or at least make things extremely difficult, as a new breed of stars emerges on the scene in the British game and look to make history.

The Ashes is the path back for both the Australian and the British game; it connects the modern game we see today with the very genesis of the sport in both countries, from 1895 to 1908. Without the Ashes, you're forsaking your roots and history and the very foundation of the code and everything that has made what the game is today.

The Ashes brings excitement, history, passion, scarcity, raw emotion and the wow event factor, something the game is still missing badly, despite the many club games in both the NRL and Super League across the regular season that will never capture the spirit and emotion like only an Ashes test series can.

The Ashes can grow the game's profile around the world

and put the British game back in the mainstream spotlight and on the back pages of newspapers, where it so deserves to be.

The Ashes will create new household stars for both the British and Australian game, become the biggest event in rugby league once again, and bring in much needed publicity and attention. It has the potential to become a financial giant for the game, just like the Ashes cricket and British and Irish Lions rugby tours are for their respective codes.

I am just a servant to the game, and the writing of this book is my way of paying this back with gratitude, and my small way of thanking the game for the incredible enjoyment over many years as a fan and admirer of the British and Australian game and past Ashes series, which fielded my love for rugby league many years ago.

My hope is for a new renaissance and revival of the greatest and most important rivalry in rugby league - The Ashes!

Best Wishes

Billy Roberts

www.ingramcontent.com/pod-product-compliance
Lightning Source LLC
Chambersburg PA
CBHW051449290426
44109CB00016B/1687